AUTHENTIC CUBAN CUISINE

AUTHENTIC CUBAN CUISINE

MARTHA ABREU CORTINA

PELICAN PUBLISHING COMPANY

GRETNA 2011

*The word "Pelican" and the depiction of a pelican
are trademarks of Pelican Publishing Company, Inc.,
and are registered in the U.S. Patent and Trademark Office.*

Library of Congress Cataloging-in-Publication Data

Cortina, Martha Abreu.
  Authentic Cuban cuisine / by Martha Abreu Cortina.
     p. cm.
  Includes index.
  ISBN 978-1-58980-955-0 (hardcover : alk. paper) 1. Cooking, Cuban. I.
Title.
  TX716.C8C67 2011
  641.597291--dc22

                                    2010052040

Printed in China
Published by Pelican Publishing Company, Inc.
1000 Burmaster Street, Gretna, Louisiana 70053

To my mother, Maria Consuelo, whose love for cooking and artful presentation of her dishes at the table inspired me to preserve her recipes, as well as those of her mother Cristina, and sisters Cuca and Maria Cristina.

The memories of my childhood in the kitchen with my mother, tasting the wonderful cakes, pies, and other delicacies she made, and those with my aunt Concha, while preparing Nochebuena, *have stayed with me to this day. I hope by sharing these family treasures with you, they will inspire new and wonderful memories to be cherished by your own families forever.*

Contents

Preface

The idea for writing this book came from years of gathering and enjoying, not just any Cuban recipe, but the best recipes from the authentic Cuban kitchen.

Over the years, I have obtained recipes from my aunts, friends, and my own mother, all of whom were particularly talented in the kitchen. They have shared their "secret" ingredients, which make these traditional recipes truly unique. Some of these I have left intact, while others I have improved with key ingredients of my own. All of these recipes have been cooked in my kitchen for years and have been sought after by my friends and family members.

Now, I share them with you, hoping that you will be inspired to try them for the enjoyment of your family and friends.

Acknowledgements

I would like to thank all those family members who have shared their recipes and expertise with me over the years, especially my sisters-in-law Irma and Clara.

Special thanks to my children Zabrina, Alonso, Juan Carlos, Lissette, and Veronique, for their support and encouragement in writing this book. Thank you, also, for your enthusiasm or constructive criticism when needed. Thanks to my five beautiful grandchildren Tyler, Gabrielle, Joshua, Adrian, and Daniel, for being my faithful "food testers," or just for being.

I would like to especially thank my husband Juan, who has been my toughest food critic, motivating me to excel and always strive for the best results in my cooking!

Important Safety Note: Pressure Cookers

In many of the following recipes, I use a pressure cooker because, over the years, it has been my best friend in the kitchen. I enjoy cooking (and eating), but why spend hours cooking a meal, if I can do it in minutes? However, it is very important to follow the safety rules of your individual pressure cooker. The cooking times start when the vent knob goes up, indicating the pressure has built inside. At this time, the heat is reduced to medium, and the counting starts. If you have a model with a different system for letting you know when the pressure has peaked, follow the manufacturer's instructions, but always count the cooking time after the pressure has peaked and you have reduced the heat to medium.

Anything that calls for a pressure cooker can also be cooked the conventional way. Simply use a good quality pot with a good lid that seals well, multiply the cooking time by two or three, and add more liquid, because it will evaporate faster with this method.

English and Spanish Recipe Ingredients

English Term	Spanish Term
Allspice	*Pimienta dulce*
Anise seeds	*Anis español*
Anise Star	*Anis Estrellado*
Bacon	*Tocino*
Basil	*Albahaca*
Bay Leaves	*Hojas de Laurel*
Bell pepper	*Aji*
Blood Sausage	*Morcilla*
Chives	*Cebollines*
Cinnamon	*Canela*
Cloves	*Clavo de Olor*
Collard Greens	*Berza*
Cooking wine	*Vino seco*
Coriander	*Cilantro*
Cumin	*Comino*
Cured, salted pork fat*	*Unto*
Dill	*Eneldo*
Garlic cloves	*Dientes de ajo*
Green onion	*Cebollines*
Ham hocks	*Lacon*
Mint	*Hierba buena*
Nutmeg	*Nuez moscada*
Onion	*Cebolla*
Oregano	*Oregano*
Paprika	*Pimenton*
Parsley	*Perejil*
Red pepper	*Pimienta roja*
Rosemary	*Romero*
Saffron	*Azafran (bijol)*
Sautee	*Sofreir*

Sour orange	*Naranja agria*
Spanish sausage	*Chorizo*
Spices	*Condimentos*
Sweet red pimentos	*Pimientos morrones*
Thyme	*Tomillo*
Turnip	*Nabo*
Turnip Greens	*Acelga*

*If *Unto* is not available, use cured, smoked bacon.

Appetizers and Salads

Cod Fish Fritters
Frituras de Bacalao

Serves 4 to 5 (4 fritters each)

1 lb. salted cod fish, dry packed
½ medium onion, chopped
¼ green bell pepper, chopped
3 tbsp. parsley, finely chopped
1 cup flour
1 egg
½ tsp. baking powder or soda
Dash black pepper
Cooking oil enough to fry

Soak the cod fish in water for about 15 minutes. Discard the water and soak fish for one more hour in fresh water. Save ½ cup of the salted fish water for later in the recipe, and discard the rest. Put fresh water in a pot, and boil the cod fish over medium heat until tender (about 35 minutes). Let cool and drain. In a food processor, place the onions, green pepper, and parsley, and chop until almost pureed. Shred the fish, add the puree from the food processor and the flour, wetting it with the salted water as necessary. Mix in the egg, baking powder, olive oil, and black pepper. Blend everything with a fork or spoon. Shape the fritters with a spoon and fry them in hot oil (350 degrees), until golden brown. Place in paper towels to drain excess oil, and serve.

Note: For flatter and "meatier" fritters, do not use baking powder.

Variation: Beef Fritters

Follow the recipe above, but replace the cod fish with ¾ lb. fresh, lean ground beef; omit the baking powder and the tbsp. of olive oil; and reduce the flour to ½ cup only. All the other ingredients remain the same. In the preparation process, place the fresh, ground beef (uncooked) in a large bowl, and add the puree from the mini food processor, the egg, the flour, black pepper, and 1 tsp. of salt. Mix well by hand, then form the fritter patties. Fry them as indicated in the recipe above.

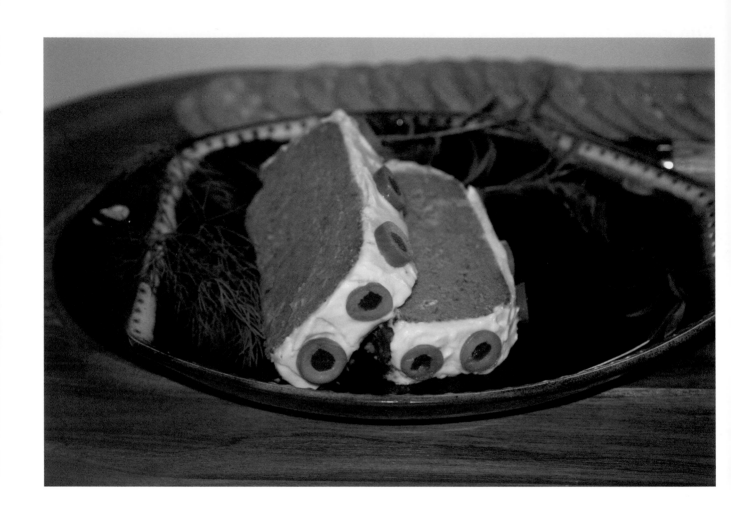

Tuna Loaf
Salpicon de Tuna

This is a wonderful party dish, which can be prepared a day or two ahead of time.

Serves 6 to 8

1 small onion, cut in chunks
1 egg
1 can red pimentos with liquid
  (7 oz.)
3 cans solid white tuna (7 oz.
  each)
3 slices bread, soaked in milk
1 tbsp. tomato puree or paste
Salt to taste
Dash cumin powder
Dash black pepper
¾ cup cracker meal
Pimento-stuffed olives, cut in half
  (for garnish)
Sliced red pimentos (for garnish)
Mayonnaise (for garnish)

In a food processor, chop the onions, egg, and can of red pimentos. Transfer to a large bowl. Drain the tuna and place in food processor; add the bread soaked in milk, tomato puree or paste, and the spices. Remember, tuna is already salted. Blend until smooth. Mix with the puree in the bowl. Add the cracker meal to give it consistency. Bake in a greased, glass loaf pan, in a 350 degree oven for about 50 minutes, or until a knife comes out clean when inserted in the center. Let cool, and invert on a serving tray. Cover with mayonnaise and decorate with sliced pimento-stuffed olives and red pimentos, inserting them into the mayonnaise. Refrigerate before serving. Serve with crackers.

Portabella and Shrimp-Filled Pastries
Camarones/Portabella en Hojaldre

Serves 6

1 box frozen pastry baskets (6 pastries)
4 tbsp. (½ stick) unsalted butter
½ red onion, chopped
5 large cloves garlic, mashed
¾ cup Portabella mushrooms, sliced and cut in half
½ lb. shrimp, peeled and cleaned
Dash dry oregano
1 tsp. salt
Dash freshly ground black pepper
¼ cup dry sherry (more if needed)
1 tbsp. flour
¼ cup milk (more if needed)

Bake pastries following directions on the package. In a large skillet, melt the butter and sauté the onion, garlic, and mushrooms for about 1 minute. Add the shrimp, seasonings, and the sherry. Cook for about 5 minutes, turning constantly with a wooden spatula. Add the flour, and keep turning to dissolve it. Add the milk, a little at a time, to smooth out the mixture, and remove from the heat. Fill each pastry and replace the "lid." Any extra shrimp and mushroom mix can be served next to the pastry shells.

Variation: Spinach Filling

3 tbsp. unsalted butter
3 tbsp. chopped onions
1 heaping tbps. flour
1 cup milk
Dash white pepper
Dash salt, to taste
2 cups steamed spinach, chopped

Bake pastries as directed on package. In a medium sauce pot, melt the butter and sauté the onions. Add the flour and stir until it separates from the sides. Add the milk, white pepper, and salt to taste. Keep stirring until smooth and thick. Remove from the heat and add the spinach, mixing everything well. Fill each pastry shell with the mixture, and replace the lid.

Ground Corn Wrap with Pork Filling
Tamal En Hoja

The main ingredient, "ground, young, tender corn" is available in the U.S. in cities where there is a large Cuban population in "natural fruit stores" (*fruterias*). You can also buy young, tender corn and grind it at home.

Yields 8 to 10 tamales

3 tbsp. cooking oil (or pork lard)
1 large onion, finely chopped
¼ green and red bell peppers, finely chopped
5 large garlic cloves, mashed
1 lb. lean pork, cut in small cubes
2 tbsp. tomato puree (or paste)
2 tsp. salt (more might be needed)
¼ tsp. cumin powder
Dash oregano
Dash crushed red pepper
¼ cup red wine or cooking wine
2 lbs. ground, young, tender corn (*maiz tierno*)
8 to 10 maize wraps (fresh or dry). Heavy aluminum foil can be used instead.*

In a large (4 or 6 qt.) saucepot, heat the oil, and sauté the onions, bell peppers, garlic, and the pork meat for approximately 2 minutes, turning constantly and cooking the meat on all sides. Add the tomato puree, the salt, and the spices. Add the wine, and reduce the heat to "low." Cover and cook for approximately 30 minutes, or until the meat is tender.

Place the ground corn in a large bowl. Stir in a tsp. of salt. Take one corn wrap, with one end folded, and fill it with the corn mixture, leaving some space in the top. Open the center with a knife or finger, and fill it with the pork mixture. Add a little more corn at the end, and place another wrap on top to close. Tie the wrapped tamal with a cooking string or cord across and lengthwise. Fill a large stock pot halfway with water, add approximately 3 tbsp. of salt, and bring the water to a boil. Place the wrapped "tamales" in the boiling water, and cook in medium/high heat, for about 45 minutes. Drain and cut the strings to serve.

*If unable to use real corn wraps to make the tamales, make a rectangular wrap with heavy aluminum foil, by folding the sides several times to avoid opening while boiling. Fold three sides leaving the top open to fill, then fold the end 2 to 3 times to close the tamal. It should measure approximately 5 inches long, by 2 ½ inches wide.

Variation: Easy Preparation

When the pork is cooked, mix the ground corn with the meat. Fill the wraps all the way up with the corn/pork mixture. This easier version is more commonly used.

Stuffed Potatoes
Papa Rellena

Serves 6 to 8

6 to 8 large potatoes, peeled and
    cut in chunks
1 tbsp. salt
1 lb. *Picadillo* (cooked ground
    beef; recipe found in the Pork,
    Beef, and Other Meats section)
1 or 2 eggs, beaten
Cracker meal for breading
Cooking oil to deep fry

Boil potatoes in water and salt until tender. Drain and mash without adding anything else. The mashed potatoes should be heavy in texture. With clean hands, shape the mashed potatoes into 3-inch balls. Poke a hole with your thumb in one side of the ball, and stuff it with 1 tbsp. of *picadillo*. Cover the hole with more mashed potatoes, and shape it, packing it well. Pass the balls through the beaten eggs first, then through the cracker meal. Fry them in enough hot oil to almost cover them. Be careful when turning them, because they can separate if not handled with care. Place on paper towels to soak up excess oil, and serve warm.

Ham or Chicken Croquettes
Croquetas de Jamon/Pollo

This popular Cuban treat is always present at birthday parties and all family gatherings. Children of all ages love *croquetas*.

Yields 16 to 20 croquettes

Béchamel Sauce
3 tbsp. butter
2 tbsp. finely chopped onion
3 heaping tbsp. flour (about ½ cup)
1 cup milk
½ tsp. salt
Dash white pepper

Ham or Chicken Croquettes
2 lbs. ground ham or ground, boiled chicken breast
4 tbsp. finely chopped parsley
Dash garlic salt
Prepared béchamel sauce
2 eggs, beaten
Cracker meal or breadcrumbs
Cooking oil to deep fry

To prepare **Béchamel Sauce**, in small pot, melt the butter and sauté the onion briefly. Add the flour at once and turn constantly until the mixture forms into a ball. Add the milk and salt and pepper; keep turning until it thickens. This béchamel should have a very thick consistency, because it is to be combined with the ground meat to form the croquettes.

To prepare **Ham or Chicken Croquettes,** mix the first 4 ingredients in a large bowl. Shape them into croquettes (about 3-inch long by 1-inch-thick cylinders). Pass each croquette through the beaten egg mixture and then through the cracker meal. Deep fry them in hot oil until golden brown. Place in paper towels to soak up excess oil.

Note: For thicker and crispier breading, pass the croquettes through the cracker meal first, then the egg, and then through the cracker meal again.

Variation: Cheese Croquettes
Follow the recipe above, replacing the 2 lbs. of ground ham with 1 ½ lbs. shredded, light-yellow cheese (such as Gouda, brick, or provolone). Everything else in the recipe stays the same.

Potato Croquettes
Croquetas de Papas

These croquettes are a favorite of many children. Great as a snack or lunch.

Yields 6 to 8 croquettes

Béchamel Sauce
2 tbsp. butter
3 generous tbsp. flour
¾ cup milk
Dash salt and white pepper

Potato Croquettes
2 lbs. potatoes, peeled
½ cup shredded yellow cheese
 (Gouda, Swiss, or Gruyere are
 best)
3 egg yolks
3 tbsp. finely chopped parsley
Dash salt and white pepper
Prepared béchamel sauce
2 eggs, beaten
Cracker meal or breadcrumbs
Cooking oil for deep frying

To prepare **Béchamel Sauce,** melt the butter in a small pot. Add the flour at once and turn constantly until the mixture forms into a ball. Add the milk and the salt and pepper; keep turning until it thickens. This Béchamel should have a very thick consistency because it is to be combined with the other ingredients to form the croquettes.

To prepare **Potato Croquettes,** cut the potatoes into chunks, and boil in salted water until tender (about 20 minutes). Drain the potatoes and place them in a large bowl. Mash them without adding any water. Mix in the rest of the ingredients, and blend together completely.

Shape this mixture into croquettes (about 3-inch-long by 1-inch-thick cylinder). If the mixture is too soft to shape, place in the refrigerator for a couple of hours and try again. Pass each croquette through the cracker meal, then through the beaten egg mixture, and back through the cracker meal again. Deep fry them in hot oil until golden brown. Place in paper towels to soak up excess oil.

Tuna in Tomato Sauce
Fritada de Tuna

This is a quick and delicious appetizer to accompany your favorite drinks and to share with friends!

Serves 6 (approximately)

3 to 4 tbsp. olive oil
½ medium onion, cut in slices
3 tbsp. tomato paste
3 cans tuna, drained (6 oz. each)
Dash oregano
Dash cumin powder
Dash black pepper
¼ cup cooking wine or dry white
   wine

In a large skillet, heat the oil and add the onion slices. Sauté, turning a few times. Add the tomato paste and the tuna, and sauté while flaking the meat. Add the spices and the wine, and keep cooking for about 3 to 4 minutes or until the wine has almost evaporated. Keep turning while cooking to prevent sticking. Can be served hot or cold. Serve with crackers.

Ham and Cream Cheese Rolls

Rollitos de Jamon

Yields 16 to 18 rolls

1 lb. sliced ham
1 softened cream cheese or Neuf-
     châtel (8 oz.)
1 to 1½ cup pitted dates or prunes

Spread cream cheese on each slice of ham (the slices can be cut in half lengthwise), place 1 date (or prune) on slice, and roll the ham. Place a toothpick through the roll to hold in place, and chill.

Five-Layer Bean Dip
Entremes En Cinco Capas

This is another party favorite. Serve with tortilla or corn chips.

Serves 6 (approximately)

- 2 large cream cheeses or Neuf-châtel (8 oz. each)
- 1 cup sliced black olives
- 1 large can refried beans, Mexican style (15 oz.)
- 2 cups chunky tomato salsa, Mexican style
- 1 lb. shredded blend of four Mexican cheeses

In a medium glass pan (8" by 8" or similar), spread the cream cheese to cover the bottom of the dish. Follow with the black olive slices, the refried beans, and the salsa. Lastly, sprinkle with the shredded cheeses. Bake in 350 degree oven until the cheese melts. Serve warm. If the cheese gets hard, reheat as needed.

Note: Dip can be reheated in a microwave.

Sandwich Spread
Pasta de Bocaditos

This is the traditional spread used to fill the tiny buns, called *bocaditos,* served at every Cuban birthday party.

Serves 10 to 12

1 lb. ground ham
¾ cup deviled ham
8 oz. cream cheese (I prefer Neuf-
  châtel)
1 can red pimentos in liquid (7 oz.)

Place all the ingredients, including the liquid from the pimentos, in a food processor and blend until smooth. Use the spread to fill small buns, Hawaiian rolls, or any other soft bun. You can also fill 2 white bread slices, peeling the outer rim, and cutting the sandwiches in half diagonally. This is a children's favorite.

Cold Meat
Carne Fria

This is a very versatile dish. It can be prepared far in advance, and refrigerated until needed. It is great to take to the beach, picnic, or a party.

Serves 10 to 12

1 onion, cut in chunks
4 garlic cloves, peeled
¼ green or red bell pepper
3 slices bread, soaked in evaporated milk
1 lb. ground ham
1 lb. lean ground beef (or ½ lb. pork and ½ lb. beef)
1 tsp. salt
¼ tsp. cumin powder
Dash black pepper
2 eggs, plus 1 beaten egg for breading
Cracker meal

Put the onions, garlic, bell pepper, eggs, and the bread soaked in milk in a blender. Blend at a low speed until smooth. Place the ground meats in a large bowl, and pour the mixture onto it. Add the salt, cumin, and black pepper. Knead with your hands thoroughly while sprinkling in cracker meal to give it consistency. Form into a 8" x 2" roll. Pass the roll through the beaten egg, then through the cracker meal. Wrap in heavy aluminum foil, sealing the edges by folding the foil together several times. Fold the ends the same way. Wrap again with the seals to the other side. Cook in a pressure cooker in about 2 inches of water for about 40 minutes (count the minutes after the pressure is built). Cool completely before unwrapping. Chill before serving. This recipe keeps in the refrigerator for several days. Serve sliced, over crackers.

Conventional Cooking Method
Prepare the meat and ingredients as above, wrapping in foil. Place the wrapped meat in a large Dutch oven or large stockpot in 3 inches of water, cover the pot, and boil over medium/high heat for 1½ hours.

Meat Pastries
Empanadillas de Picadillo

This recipe is made with *Picadillo,* which is found in the Pork, Beef, and Other Meats section.

Yields about 8 to 10 meat pastries

6 tbsp. milk
3 tbsp. cooking oil
½ tsp. salt
12 tbsp. flour
½ lb. prepared *Picadillo* (see the Pork, Beef, and Other Meats section for recipe)

In a large bowl, mix the milk, oil, and salt. Add the flour a little at a time, blending completely, but do not knead. Cover with plastic wrap, and let stand for 30 minutes. Knead the dough well and form a roll. Cut into 2 or 3 inch sections, and roll out with rolling pin, forming a flat disk, about 5 inches wide. Fill each one with a tablespoon of *Picadillo* in the center. Wet the outside rim and fold, pressing down with a fork to seal. Deep fry in hot oil. Drain on paper towels.

Beef Dome
Domo de Carne

Serves 6 to 8

1 bunch green onions (chives)
¾ cup dry beef slices (found in the canned meat section)
1 large cream cheese, regular or Neufchâtel (8 oz.)
Dash black pepper
½ cup sliced almonds or chopped walnuts

Chop the green part of the green onions and discard the white portion. Cut the beef into small sections. Place the beef and the green onions in a food processor. Cut the cream cheese into chunks and add to the food processor; add black pepper and process until smooth. Using your hands or a wide knife, shape into a dome (or ball), and press the almonds or walnuts over the entire dome to cover completely. Serve with crackers.

Bacon and Date Rolls
Rollitos de Bacon y Datiles

Yields 16 to 18 rolls

1 to 1½ cup dry dates
1 lb. sliced bacon
Toothpicks

Place a date at the end of each slice of bacon, and roll up completely. Use a toothpick to hold the bacon in place. Bake in 350 degree oven for approximately 25 minutes, or until bacon is crisp. Let them drain in paper towels before serving.

Variation: Bacon and Chestnuts
Replace the dates with canned chestnuts, rolled in brown sugar. Roll each slice of bacon with one chestnut inside. Bake the same way.

Swiss Cheese Fondue
Derretido de Queso Suizo

This is a favorite party dish. It looks sophisticated and tastes wonderful.

Serves 10 to 12

2 cups natural Swiss cheese, shredded
2 cups shredded Gruyère cheese (**)
1 tbsp. cornstarch
1 garlic clove, cut into halves
1 cup dry white wine (Pinot Grigio)
1 tbsp. lemon juice
3 tbsp. kirsch or dry sherry
½ tsp. salt
⅛ tsp. white pepper
French or Cuban bread, toasted and cut into 1-inch pieces

Toss cheese with cornstarch until coated. Rub garlic on bottom and sides of heavy saucepan or skillet, and add wine. Heat over low heat just until bubbles rise to the surface; wine should not boil. Stir in lemon juice. Gradually add cheeses, about ½ cup at a time, stirring constantly with wooden spoon over low heat until cheeses are melted. Stir in kirsch (or sherry), salt, and white pepper. Transfer to fondue dish and keep warm over low heat. Serve with toasted bread.

Note: If fondue becomes thick, stir in ¼ to ½ cup of heated wine. **You can substitute 2 additional cups of Swiss cheese for the Gruyère if desired.

Seafood Salad
Ensalada de Mariscos

Yields 8 to 10 small servings

1 lb. crab meat (or imitation crab meat)
2 celery stalks, chopped
2 hard boiled eggs, chopped
1 large apple, cored and cut into small cubes
¼ onion, chopped (I prefer white onion for this recipe)
2 tbsp. ketchup
Dash salt and black pepper
¼ cup mayonnaise (light or regular)

Flake the crab meat with 2 forks. Add all the ingredients until well mixed. You can add more mayonnaise, if desired. Serve on crackers, or for a more creative look, serve on lettuce leaves or inside clam shells.

Note: I save the shells from clams used for seafood dishes, wash and dry them, and then store them for later use at parties for serving this salad.

Traditional Chicken Salad
Ensalada de Pollo Tradicional

This is the traditional chicken salad served at the Cuban birthday parties of yesteryear.

Serves 16 to 18

8 chicken breasts
2 large potatoes, peeled and cut into ½-inch cubes
¼ white onion, cut in chunks
2 cans sweet, red pimentos (7 oz.) with 1 can set aside for decorating
2 Red Delicious apples, peeled, cored, and cut into cubes
3 boiled eggs (1 set aside for decorating)
2 small (8 oz.) cans sweet peas (Petit Pois)
Dash black pepper
Mayonnaise to taste
Salt to taste
1 can white or green asparagus for decorating (can use both types)

Boil the chicken breasts in salted water until tender. Let cool, and take off the skin and the bones from the chicken, saving the broth for another recipe. Boil the potatoes in a separate pot, until they are cooked through, but not too tender; you do not want them to get mashed. When they are just right, drain the potatoes and put them in cold water to stop the cooking process. In a large bowl, shred the chicken meat by hand or with 2 forks. Place the onion and 1 can of red pimentos in a blender and puree. Pour the mix onto the chicken meat, and toss to blend. Add the apples; 2 boiled eggs, chopped; the sweet peas; the black pepper; and enough mayonnaise to hold everything together. Check the salt, and add more if necessary. Fold in the potatoes carefully to keep them from breaking apart. Transfer to a serving dish, and decorate with the asparagus, slices of red pimento, and 1 boiled egg, thinly sliced.

Fruit Cocktail Salad
Ensalada de Cocktel de Frutas

Serves 6 to 8

2 large cans fruit cocktail, drained
   (28 oz. each)
½ head iceberg lettuce, chopped
¾ cup chopped walnuts
Salt and pepper to taste
Mayonnaise (light or regular)

Mix all the ingredients with enough mayonnaise to hold them together. Serve cold as a side dish or party treat. For a more decorative display, serve inside lettuce leaves.

Crushed Pineapple and Cream Cheese Salad
Ensalada de Piña con Queso Crema

Serves 4

1 can crushed pineapple (20 oz.)
½ 8 oz. cream cheese (Neufchâtel is creamier and has less fat)
1 carrot, grated
1 apple, cored and cut into small cubes (or chopped)
1 box raisins (1½ oz.)
1 tbsp. sugar

Strain the crushed pineapple, and use some of the juice to soften the cream cheese in a medium bowl. Add the strained pineapples, and the rest of the ingredients together, folding them in carefully. Chill before serving.

Note: I recommend grating the carrot with a hand grater. It comes out softer and juicier.

Soups and Beans

Black Beans
Frijoles Negros

This is the most "Cuban" of all the bean dishes, and definitely the most popular and loved by all.

Serves 4 to 6 as a soup

1 bag dry black beans (14 oz.)
¼ lb. bacon, cut in cubes
1 medium yellow or Vidalia onion, chopped
½ green and ½ red bell peppers, cut in 4 pieces
6 large garlic cloves, mashed
1 tbsp. salt
1 large coriander (cilantro) leaf, chopped
3 bay leaves
½ tsp. sugar
¼ tsp. cumin powder (more can be used if desired)
¼ tsp. dry oregano leaves, crushed
½ white onion, pureed in food processor
1 can sweet red pimento with liquid (7 oz.)
3 tbsp. vinegar
3 tbsp. olive oil

Soak the beans in water for approximately 10 hours.

In a pressure cooker,* fry the bacon (in medium/high heat) until it has shed some fat, and it begins to look golden but not crispy. Add the yellow onion, bell peppers, and garlic, and sauté with the bacon until the onions are transparent. Add the black beans, and enough water to cover 2 inches above the beans. Add the salt, coriander, bay leaves, sugar, and the rest of the spices.

Cover the cooker and wait for the pressure to build. Reduce the heat to medium and cook for 35 minutes. When the pressure is gone, open the cooker, and check the soup. If it is not thick, simmer the soup, uncovered, in low heat until some of the liquid evaporates.

When soup has the proper consistency, remove from the heat, and add the pureed white onion, the can of red pimentos (sliced or pureed), the vinegar, and the olive oil. Stir all these ingredients into the soup. Simmer for another 5 to 10 minutes. Serve over white rice, or alone as a soup. (I puree the white onion with the can of sweet red pimentos in a blender. However, the can of pimentos can be omitted; increase the sugar to 1 tsp. and increase the vinegar.)

*Conventional Cooking Method

After soaking the beans, use a 5 to 6 qt. Dutch oven or large stockpot, and follow the directions to prepare the bacon, onion, peppers, and spices. Next, add beans and water to the stockpot or Dutch oven, bring the beans to a boil, reduce the heat to medium/high, and partially cover. Do not cover completely to allow the steam to escape. Cook for 1½ to 2 hours, or until the beans are tender. Check often, and add more water if necessary, but keep in mind that this soup should be thick. Add pureed onion, red pimentos, vinegar, and olive oil as above.

Red Kindey Bean Soup
Frijoles Colorados

Serves 4 to 6

1 bag dry, red kidney beans (14 or 16 oz.)
2 or 3 pieces smoked ham hocks
1 tsp. salt
3 tbsp. olive oil
1 large onion, chopped
½ green bell pepper, chopped
5 to 6 large garlic cloves, mashed
1 Spanish sausage cut into ½-inch pieces
1 tbsp. tomato paste
½ lb. Cuban-style pumpkin (calabaza), peeled and cut into large chunks
1 large potato, peeled and cut into chunks
¼ tsp. cumin powder
¼ tsp. crushed dry oregano leaves
2 bay leaves
1 yellow/green plantain (optional)

Soak the dry beans overnight, or for 10 hours, in enough water to cover the beans by 2 inches. After they have soaked, transfer them to a large pressure cooker,* with the water left in the beans, plus 2 more inches of water. Add the ham hocks and 1 tsp. of salt, and cook for 25 to 30 minutes.

In the meantime, heat the olive oil in a skillet. Add the onions, bell peppers, garlic, and Spanish sausage. Sauté until the onions are transparent. Add the tomato paste, and stir to combine everything. Turn off the heat.

When the beans are finished cooking, open the pressure cooker (when the pressure is gone), and add the ingredients from the skillet. Stir together. Add the calabaza (pumpkin), potato, and the spices to the cooker, and stir together. Check the salt and the liquid, and add more if necessary. Simmer in medium/low heat for another 30 minutes covered with a lid from a regular pot, *not* the pressure cooker lid. If the liquid has not thickened or if it has too much liquid, mash a few of the potato chunks, and simmer the soup for a few more minutes, uncovered.

Variation: Plantains

While the beans are simmering, heat cooking oil in a deep fryer, and cut the yellow/green plantain into 1-inch pieces. Fry the plantain in the oil until tender. Place the fried plantains on paper towels to soak up the excess oil. Flatten each piece by covering it with a folded paper towel and pressing down with your hand, or use a Cuban-style *tostonera*. Add the plantains to the beans before serving.

*Conventional Cooking Method

After soaking the beans, transfer the beans and soaking water to a 5 to 6 qt. Dutch oven or large stockpot. Cover the beans with water, plus 2 inches more. Add the ham hocks and 1 tsp. of salt. Bring to a boil, reduce the heat to medium/high, and partially cover, to allow steam to escape. Cook for 1½ to 2 hours, or until the beans are tender. Check often, and add more water if necessary. Continue with the rest of the recipe above.

Lentil Soup
Lentejas

Serves 4 to 6

1 bag dry lentil beans (14 or 16 oz.)
2 or 3 pieces smoked ham hocks
3 tbsp. olive oil
1 large onion, chopped
1 tbsp. tomato paste
½ green bell pepper, chopped
5 garlic cloves, mashed
1 sweet potato, peeled and cut into large chunks
1 large potato, peeled and cut into large chunks
¼ tsp. cumin powder
¼ tsp. crushed dry oregano leaves
Salt to taste

Soak the dry beans for 1 hour in enough water to cover the beans by 2 inches. Cook the ham hocks for 30 minutes in the pressure cooker* with about 3 cups of water. Begin timing after the pressure has peaked, and the cooker has been turned to medium heat. Heat the oil in a skillet; add the onions, tomato paste, green pepper, and garlic. Sauté until the onions are transparent. Remove from heat.

After the ham hocks are cooked and the pressure is gone, open the cooker and add the lentils with the water, plus enough additional water to cover them. Add the ingredients from the skillet, the potatoes, and the spices. Check the taste, and add salt if necessary. Close the pressure cooker, wait for the pressure to peak, and cook for 25 minutes on medium to low heat. When the pressure is gone, open the cooker and stir the lentils gently. If the liquid is not thick enough, mash a few potatoes and simmer the soup, uncovered, for a few more minutes.

*Conventional Cooking Method
Cook the ham hocks in a 5 to 6 qt. Dutch oven or stockpot in 4 cups of water. Bring the water to a boil, and reduce the heat to medium, cooking the ham for 1½ hours. Heat the oil in a skillet, and add the onions, tomato paste, green bell pepper, and garlic. Sauté until the onions are transparent. Remove from heat, and add to the ham hocks in the stockpot. Add the lentils with the soaking water, plus enough water to cover the lentils. Add the spices and potatoes. Check the salt, and add more if necessary. Bring to a boil, reduce the heat to medium-high, and cook for 1 to 1½ hours, or until the lentils are tender.

Spanish White Bean Potage

Fabada

This recipe is an authentic Spanish dish, which has been adopted in Cuban cuisine.

Serves 4 to 6

1 bag white, broad beans (14 oz.)
1 tbsp. salt
3 tbsp. olive oil
1 large onion, chopped
6 garlic cloves, crushed
½ green bell pepper, chopped
1 tbsp. tomato puree
½ lb. smoked ham hocks
2 blood sausages (*morcilla*), cut in slices**
1 Spanish sausage, cut in ¼-inch slices**
¼ lb. bacon, cut into 1-inch pieces
1 large potato, peeled and cut in small chunks
¼ tsp. cumin powder
¼ tsp. dried oregano leaves
¼ tsp. paprika
Dash black pepper

Wash beans well. Soak in water for about 10 hours. In a pressure cooker,* cover the beans with water by 2 inches, add the salt, and cook for 30 minutes in medium heat after the pressure valve goes up.

In the meantime, heat olive oil in a smaller pot, or skillet. Add onions, garlic, green peppers, tomato puree, and all the meats. Sauté until the onions are golden brown. Turn off the heat. When the beans are cooked, wait until all the pressure is gone, and open the cooker.

*Turn the heat in the pressure cooker to medium; add the meat sauce and the rest of the ingredients (potato chunks and spices). Check the salt, and add more if necessary. Simmer, covered with a regular lid and not the pressure cooker lid, on medium-low heat until the soup thickens, about 30 to 45 minutes.

Note: If you prefer, take the skin off the blood sausages and the Spanish sausage, and crumble the meat inside. **Spanish sausages are typically 4 to 5 inches long and *morcilla* is typically 3 to 4 inches long.

*Conventional Cooking Method

After soaking the beans, transfer the beans and water to a 5 to 6 qt. Dutch oven or large stockpot. Add enough water to cover the beans by 3 inches. Add the salt, and bring to a boil. Reduce the heat to medium-high, and partially cover, to allow steam to escape. Cook for 1½ hours or until the beans are tender. Check often, and add more water if necessary. Continue with the recipe above, from the second asterisk.

Galician White Bean Soup

Caldo Gallego

This is another authentic recipe from Spain, which found its way into Cuban cuisine.

Serves 4 to 6

1 bag dry, white navy beans (14 oz.)
3 tbsp. olive oil
1 large onion, chopped
5 garlic cloves, mashed
½ green bell pepper, chopped
¼ lb. cooking ham, cut in small chunks
¼ lb. bacon, cut in small chunks
¼ lb. *unto* (salt-cured pork fat) cut in chunks
1 Spanish sausage (chorizo), cut in slices
1 bunch collard greens
1 large potato, peeled and cut in big chunks
1 turnip, peeled and cut in chunks
1 tbsp. salt
¼ tsp. cumin powder
¼ tsp. dried oregano leaves, crushed
¼ tsp. paprika

Wash beans, cover with water, and soak for approximately 10 hours. In the pressure cooker,* heat the olive oil. Add the onions, garlic, peppers, ham, bacon, *unto,* and Spanish sausage. Sauté until onions are transparent. Wash the collard greens and cut the leaves into small sections; do not use the base of the greens. Add it to the meats in the cooker.

Add the beans with the water they soaked in to the cooker, along with the potato, turnip, salt, and spices. Add enough water to cover the ingredients by 3 inches. Close the cooker and wait until the pressure has built with the heat on high. Lower the heat to medium, and cook for 35 minutes. When the pressure is gone, open the cooker and check the beans for tenderness, being careful not to mash the potatoes. Check the soup for taste, and add more salt if necessary. This soup should be very watery, not thick. You might want to remove some of the beans to make a true *Galician Caldo.* If you want a more Cuban soup, leave all the beans.

Note: You can use aged, cured, smoked bacon—not the sliced variety—in place of *unto.*

*Conventional Cooking Method

After soaking the beans, use a 5 to 6 qt. Dutch oven or large stockpot, and follow the recipe above. After adding all the ingredients to the pot, bring to a boil, reduce the heat to medium-high, and partially cover, to allow the steam to escape. Cook for 1½ to 2 hours, or until the beans are tender. Check often, and add more water if necessary.

White Bean Potage

Potage de Frijoles Blancos

Serves 6

1 bag dry, white navy beans (14 or 16 oz.)
1 tbsp. salt
3 tbsp. olive oil
1 large onion, chopped
½ cup green and/or red bell pepper, chopped
6 to 7 large garlic cloves, mashed
1 Spanish sausage (chorizo), cut into slices
¼ lb. smoked ham, cut into chunks
2 tbsp. tomato paste
¼ cup cooking wine
1 large potato, peeled and cut into chunks
¼ to ½ lb. calabaza (Cuban pumpkin), cut into chunks (If unavailable, sliced carrots may be used instead)
¼ tsp. cumin powder
Dash oregano
Dash paprika
Dash black pepper
Salt to taste

Soak the dry beans overnight, or for 10 hours, in enough water to cover the beans by 2 inches. Afterwards, place the beans and water in a pressure cooker,* add enough water to cover the beans by 2 inches, add 1 tbsp. of salt, and cook for 30 minutes. Always start counting after the pressure has built, and the heat reduced to medium.

In the meantime, heat the olive oil in a skillet. Add the onions, bell peppers, garlic, Spanish sausages, and smoked ham. Sauté until onions are transparent. Add the tomato paste and the cooking wine, stir to combine everything, and turn off the heat. When the beans are finished cooking and the pressure is gone, open the pressure cooker (or stock pot), and add the ingredients from the skillet; stir together. Add the potatoes, calabaza, and the rest of the ingredients (spices), and stir together. Check the salt and the liquid, and add more if necessary. Cover and simmer everything on medium-low heat for another 25 minutes. Use a lid from a regular pot, *not* the pressure cooker lid. If the liquid has not thickened or if it has too much liquid, mash a few of the potato chunks, and simmer the soup for a few more minutes, uncovered.

*Conventional Cooking Method

After soaking the beans, transfer the beans and water to a 5 to 6 qt. Dutch oven or large stockpot. Add enough water to cover the beans by 3 inches. Add the salt, and bring to a boil. Reduce the heat to medium-high, and partially cover, to allow the steam to escape. Cook for 1½ to 2 hours, or until the beans are tender. Check often, and add more water if necessary. Continue with the recipe above, beginning with the onions, bell peppers, garlic, and Spanish sausage in the skillet.

Chickpea Soup
Potage de Garbanzo

Serves 4 to 6

1 bag dry chickpeas (14 or 16 oz.)
1 tbps. salt
3 tbsp. olive oil
1 large onion, chopped
½ green bell pepper, chopped
5 large garlic cloves, mashed
2 Spanish sausages (chorizo), cut in slices
2 tbsp. tomato paste
¼ cup cooking wine
1 large potato, peeled and cut in chunks
½ cabbage, cut up in 2-inch chunks
¼ tsp. paprika
¼ tsp. cumin powder
Dash oregano
Salt to taste
Dash crushed red pepper (optional)

Soak the dry beans overnight, or for 10 hours, in enough water to cover the beans by 2 inches. Afterwards, place the beans and water in a pressure cooker,* add enough water to cover them by 2 inches, add 1 tbsp. of salt, and cook for 30 minutes. Always start counting after the pressure has built, and the heat reduced to medium.

*In the meantime, heat the olive oil in a skillet. Add the onions, bell peppers, garlic, and Spanish sausages. Sauté until onions are transparent. Add the tomato paste and the cooking wine, stir to combine everything, and turn off the heat. When the beans are finished cooking, open the pressure cooker after the pressure is gone, and add the ingredients from the skillet; stir together. Add the potatoes, cabbage, and the rest of the ingredients (spices), and stir together. Check the salt and the liquid, and add more if necessary. Cover and simmer everything in medium to low heat for another 30 minutes. Use a lid from a regular pot, *not* the pressure cooker lid. If the liquid has not thickened or if it has too much liquid, mash a few of the potato chunks, and simmer the soup for a few more minutes, uncovered.

*Conventional Cooking Method

After soaking the beans, transfer the beans and water to a 5 to 6 qt. Dutch oven or large stockpot. Add enough water to cover the beans by 3 inches. Add the salt, and bring to a boil. Reduce the heat to medium-high, and partially cover, to allow the steam to escape. Cook for 1½ to 2 hours or until the beans are tender. Check often, and add more water if necessary. Continue with the recipe above, from the second asterisk.

Split Pea Soup

Chicharos

Serves 4 to 6

1 bag dry, split peas (14 oz.)
3 tbsp. olive oil
1 medium onion, chopped
½ green pepper, chopped
5 garlic cloves, crushed
¼ lb. cooking ham
1 smoked ham hock (optional)
½ lb. Cuban-style pumpkin (calabaza) peeled and cut into chunks
1 medium potato, peeled and cut into small chunks
1 carrot, cut into slices
1 tbsp. salt
¼ tsp. cumin powder
Dash oregano

Wash the split peas and soak them in water for 2 hours. In the pressure cooker,* heat the olive oil and add the onions, garlic, green pepper, and ham cut into small chunks. Sauté until the onions are golden. Add all the vegetables and spices, and sauté, turning constantly for about 1 minute. Add the peas with the water to the cooker, and add enough additional water to cover the ingredients by 2 inches.

*Close the cooker and wait until the valve goes up, indicating there is pressure. Turn down the heat to medium, and cook for 25 minutes. When the pressure is gone, open the cooker and check to see if there is too much water. Stir the soup slowly and leave on low heat to evaporate excess liquid, if necessary. If the soup is too thick, you can add a little water.

Important Safety Note: Always use a 6 qt. pressure cooker, or larger, for this amount of soup. If a smaller cooker is used, it might get clogged with the foam produced by the split peas when cooking.

*Conventional Cooking Method
After soaking the beans, use a 5 to 6 qt. Dutch oven or large stockpot, and follow the recipe above, until it calls for heating the soup in the pressure cooker. After adding all the ingredients together, bring pot to a boil, reduce the heat to medium-high, and partially cover, to allow the steam to escape. Cook for 1½ hours or until the beans are tender. Stir and check often, and add more water if necessary.

Creamy Corn Chowder with Pork

Tamal en Cazuela

This recipe calls for a very specialized ingredient available in the U.S. only in cities where there is a large Cuban population. "Ground, young, tender corn" is sold in specialized natural fruit stores or *fruterias*.

Serves 6 to 8

3 tbsp. cooking oil or pork lard
1 large onion, chopped
¼ green and red bell peppers, chopped
6 large garlic cloves, mashed
1 lb. lean pork, cut into small chunks
½ can tomato puree or paste (6 oz.)
2 tsp. salt (more might be needed)
½ tsp. cumin powder
2 bay leaves, crushed
Dash oregano
Dash crushed red pepper
¼ cup cooking wine
2 lbs. ground, young, tender corn (*maiz tierno*)

In a large 6 or 8 qt. pot, heat the oil, and sauté the onions, bell peppers, garlic, and the pork meat for about 2 minutes, turning constantly and cooking the meat on all sides. Add the tomato puree, the salt, and the spices. Add cooking wine, and lower the heat. Cover and simmer for a few more minutes, then turn off the heat.

Pour 1 cup of the ground corn with 3 cups of water into a blender, and blend until smooth. Strain this mixture, and pour it into the pot where the pork meat is. Put the pulp left in the strainer back in the blender with 1 cup of water, and blend again until smooth. Strain and pour it in the pot. Repeat this process as long as the strained liquid is "milky." You will repeat this whole process until you are finished with the entire 2 lbs. of corn.

Once all the corn has been added, check the salt and add more if needed. This is *key* to bringing out the taste. Cook the blended corn with the pork in medium-low heat, stirring occasionally, for about 1 hour or until the chowder tastes cooked, not powdery, and it has thickened.

Corn Stew

Guiso de Maiz

Serves 4 to 6

6 ears young, tender corn (water should come out when poked with fingernail)
3 tbsp. cooking oil
1 medium onion, chopped
½ green and/or red bell pepper, chopped
5 large cloves garlic, mashed
1 Spanish sausage (chorizo), cut in slices
¼ lb. cooking ham, cubed (or smoked ham hocks, with skin cut off)
1 small can tomato paste (3 tbsp.)
¼ tsp. cumin powder
½ tsp. seasoning (Sazón Goya or Sazón Accent)
Salt and black pepper to taste
1 potato, peeled and cut into small chunks
½ lb. calabaza (pumpkin), peeled and cut into chunks
2 cubes dry chicken broth
¼ cup cooking wine
1½ cups cream of corn, frozen or canned

Clean the corn and cut 3 ears into 1-inch slices. Run a sharp knife through the sides of the other 3 to cut the kernels. In a large sauce pot or Dutch oven, heat the oil and add the onions, bell peppers, garlic, chorizo, and ham (or ham hocks). Sauté for about 1 minute. Add the corn, tomato paste, cumin, and the rest of the seasonings. Sauté for another minute, turning constantly. Add the potatoes, calabaza, dry broth, and wine, and add water to cover everything. Reduce the heat, cover, and cook for about 35 minutes or until the corn is cooked. Check the salt, and add more if necessary. Add the frozen cream of corn, and simmer until the stew thickens. Some cooks will add 1 tbsp. of cornstarch, dissolved in a little water, to thicken the stew.

Chickpeas with Pigs' Feet

Garbanzos con Paticas

Serves 4 to 6

1 bag dry chickpeas (14 or 16 oz.)
2 to 3 pigs' feet, cut in 4 pieces each
1 tbsp. salt
3 tbsp. olive oil
1 large onion, chopped
½ green bell pepper, chopped
5 garlic cloves, mashed
1 Spanish sausage (chorizo), cut into slices
1 small can tomato paste (6 oz.)
¼ cup cooking wine
1 large potato, peeled and cut in chunks
½ cabbage, cut up in 2-inch sections
¼ tsp. paprika
¼ tsp. cumin powder
Dash oregano
Salt and pepper to taste
Dash crushed red pepper

Soak the dry beans overnight, or for 10 hours, in enough water to cover the beans by 2 inches. Cook the pigs' feet in about 3 cups of water and 1 tbsp. of salt in the pressure cooker* for 30 minutes. Begin timing the pigs' feet after the pressure has peaked, and the heat is reduced to medium. After the time is up and the pressure is gone, open the cooker and discard the water.

*In the meantime, heat the olive oil in a skillet. Add the onions, bell peppers, garlic, and Spanish sausage. Sauté until onions are transparent. Add the tomato paste and the cooking wine, stir to combine everything, and turn off the heat. Add the garbanzo beans to the pigs' feet in the pressure cooker or stockpot, if not using the pressure cooker. Add the ingredients from the skillet, the potatoes, the cabbage, and the rest of the ingredients (spices), and stir together. Check the salt and the liquid, and add more if necessary. There should be enough water to cover the beans by 2 inches.

Cover and cook in the pressure cooker again on medium heat for 40 minutes; always start to count after the pressure peaks. After the pressure is gone, open the pressure cooker and simmer, uncovered, on low for a few more minutes to thicken the sauce.

*Conventional Cooking Method

Use a 5 to 6 qt. Dutch oven or large stockpot. Cook the pigs' feet for about 1 hour. Discard the water. Continue with the recipe above, from the second asterisk until all the ingredients are combined. Then, bring to a boil, reduce the heat to medium, and cook for 2 hours, or until the garbanzo beans are tender, turning occasionally.

Beef and Garbanzo Soup

Sopa de Garbanzo con Ternilla de Res

This is one of my family's favorite soups. It is a complete meal in a bowl!

Serves 4 to 6

2 lbs. beef short ribs
1 large onion, cut into large chunks
½ green bell pepper
2 garlic cloves, peeled and cut in half
¼ tsp. cumin powder
1 tbsp. salt
1 large can chickpeas (garbanzo beans), packed in water and salt (19 oz.)
½ bag "angel hair" soup noodles (16 oz. bag)

Place the ribs and the next five ingredients in a pressure cooker.* Add water to cover the ribs by about 2 inches. Cover and turn the heat to high, until the pressure peaks. Lower the heat to medium, and cook for 1 hour and 15 minutes. After the pressure is gone, open the pressure cooker.

Remove the bones with a strainer, and discard. Remove as much of the onions and bell pepper from the soup as you can. Cut the big chunks of beef into more manageable sizes, or shred them a little bit. Open the can of garbanzo beans, drain the liquid, and place beans in a blender. Add a small amount of water, and puree until smooth. Add it to the soup and stir to mix. Turn the heat to high. When soup starts to boil, crush the noodles a little with your hands and place them in the soup. Boil for another 10 to 12 minutes, until the noodles are tender, turning with a large spoon often. Check the salt, and add more if necessary. If the consistency of the soup is too thick, add a little more water.

*Conventional Cooking Method

In a large Dutch oven or stockpot, place the ribs and the next five ingredients. Add enough water to cover the ribs by 3 inches. Bring to a boil, reduce the heat to medium, and cook for 2½ hours or until the meat is tender and falling off the bones. Then, follow the above recipe beginning with straining the bones from the mixture.

Calabaza Squash Cream Soup

Crema de Calabaza

Serves 4

8 cups chicken or beef broth (homemade broth highly recommeded)
2 lbs. calabaza (Cuban pumpkin) or butternut squash
Salt to taste
3 tbsp. unsalted butter
1 cup heavy cream
Dash ground nutmeg

Place the broth in a large pot with lid. Peel the calabaza or squash, and spoon out the seeds and loose threads of pulp surrounding the seeds. Rinse and cut into big chunks. Cook in the broth, over medium-high heat, for about 15 to 20 minutes or until tender. Taste for salt, and add more if necessary. Pour half of the liquid into a separate container. Using a hand blender, puree the squash with the broth left in the pot. Add more broth, a little at a time, if necessary, until mixture reaches a thick, creamy consistency. A regular blender may be used also. Simmer the creamy soup for a few more minutes, while adding the butter and the cup of cream. Serve hot. Sprinkle a little ground nutmeg on each soup after serving it.

Malanga Cream Soup

Crema de Malanga

This delicious cream soup is quickly becoming a favorite among the customers who visit Cuban restaurants in South Florida. It is very easy and inexpensive to make at home.

Serves 4

6 cups chicken broth (chicken boiled with ½ an onion, ¼ green bell pepper, and salt to taste)
4 large malanga roots (malangas are root vegetables with brown, hairy skin and white meat inside)
Salt to taste
3 tbsp. unsalted butter
1 cup heavy cream

Place the broth in a large pot with a lid. Peel the malangas and rinse them. Cut into big chunks, and cook in the broth, over medium-high heat, for about 20 minutes or until tender. Taste for salt, and add more if necessary. Pour half of the liquid into a separate container. Using a hand blender, puree the malangas with the broth left in the pot. Add more broth if necessary, until mixture reaches a thick, creamy consistency. If you need more liquid, you can add a little water. Simmer the creamy soup for a couple more minutes, while adding the butter and the cup of cream. Serve hot. Garnish with a pat of butter.

Vegetable Cream Soups
Sopas de Vegetales en Crema

Serves 4 to 6

1 lb. butternut squash (or asparagus, celery, broccoli, carrots
   or other vegetables)
8 cups chicken or beef broth
   (boiled with onions and green
   bell pepper)
Salt to taste
3 tbsp. unsalted butter
1 cup heavy cream

Prepare the vegetable according to its type: peel, wash, cut off the ends and/or take out seeds. If cooking asparagus, cut off stalks about 2 inches from the bottom. Cut the vegetable into smaller pieces, and cook in the broth for about 20 minutes or until tender. Taste for salt, and add more if necessary. In a blender, puree the vegetables with a little broth and return to the pot. Simmer for a couple more minutes while adding the butter and the cup of cream. Serve hot. Garnish with celery leaves or chopped chives.

Note: This recipe is good for a variety of different vegetables. You also can combine 2 or more of the vegetables. The asparagus, celery, and butternut squash soups are very delicate in flavor and perfect for a more sophisticated dinner. The broccoli, spinach, and carrot soups are stronger in flavor.

Fish Soup, Cuban-Style

Sopa de Cherna

Serves 4 to 6

1 grouper head or any other white fish
2 tsp. salt
1 medium onion, cut into chunks
¼ green bell pepper, cut into 4 pieces
4 to 5 garlic cloves, mashed
1 cup white rice
½ cup sliced carrots
1 potato, peeled and diced
Dash cumin powder
2 cilantro (coriander) leaves
Pinch saffron (adds color and flavor)

In a large saucepot, heat 8 cups of water. Add the fish head with the salt, onions, bell peppers, and garlic cloves. Bring to a boil, reduce the heat to medium, and cook for 20 minutes, covered. Strain the soup, and return the strained broth back to the pot. Discard the onions, peppers, and garlic. Place the fish in a bowl, and let cool. Carefully remove the meat from the head with a fork, and place the meat back in the broth, discarding the bones. Turn the heat back on. Add the rest of the ingredients. Check the taste, and add more salt if necessary. Bring the soup to a boil, then reduce the heat to medium. Simmer the soup, covered, for another 20 minutes. Remove the cilantro leaves before serving.

Green Plantain Soup

Sopa de Platano

Serves 6 to 8

Homemade Beef Broth
1 lb. beef (cut of your choice)
1 tbsp. salt
1 large piece onion
1 large piece green bell pepper
2 to 3 garlic cloves, mashed (can use more if desired)

Green Plantain Soup
2 large green plantains (or 3 medium)
Cooking oil for deep frying
8 cups homemade beef broth
Salt to taste
1 lime

To prepare the **Homemade Beef Broth,** boil 1 lb. of beef, such as skirt, short ribs, or other, in 8½ cups of water with salt, onion, green bell pepper, and garlic cloves. Reduce heat, and simmer until the meat is tender. If using a pressure cooker, cook for 45 minutes. If using conventional methods, cook for 1½ hours. Strain, and use the meat for another recipe.

To make **Green Plantain Soup**, peel the green plantains and cut them into thin slices (chips). Heat the oil in a deep fryer. When the oil is hot, fry the plantain chips until crispy but do not burn. Place the chips in a paper towel to drain excess oil. Place the chips in a food processor, and grind to make crumbs. In a large saucepot, heat the broth, and place the plantain crumbs into the broth, a little at a time, stirring constantly. Check the taste, and add more salt if necessary. Cook over medium-low heat, stirring often, until the soup is creamy and smooth. Serve immediately. Add a little lime juice to the soup after serving.

Note: To make an interesting garnish, peel 1 green plantain, and make a few long plantain chips by shaving the plantain lengthwise. Deep fry the slices in hot oil. Garnish the individual bowls of soup with 2 or 3 long plantain chips.

Cuban Vegetable and Meat Soup

Ajiaco

Ajiaco is the most traditional and popular Cuban soup. It is made from several root vegetables grown in Cuba and the Caribbean area. This soup is gaining popularity in the United States, and some famous chefs even claim to have "the best" recipe. You will need a large stock pot.

Serves 12

1 lb. Tasajo (dry, salted meat), cut in strips
5 to 6 beef ribs
1 lb. lean pork meat, cut into chunks
2 large onions, cut into chunks
5 to 6 large garlic cloves, mashed
1 green bell pepper, seeded and cut into 6 pieces
Salt to taste
¼ tsp. cumin powder
2 large yucca roots
3 to 4 malanga roots
2 large plantains (1 green and 1 yellow)
1 large cilantro leaf (the long ones or several of the round ones)
Pinch saffron
1 large ñame (if available)
4 or 5 ears young, fresh corn, peeled and cut into small sections
2 boniatos (white sweet potatoes)
½ lb. calabaza (Cuban pumpkin)
Bollitos (cornmeal nuggets)

If using the real Tasajo, which is salted, cut it into 4 to 5 sections, and soak them in water for a few hours, discarding the water several times, and do not add salt to the meats. If not using Tasajo, use 1 tbsp. of salt when cooking the meats. Place the 3 meats, the onions, garlic, green bell pepper, salt, and cumin powder with 4 to 6 cups of water in a large 6 to 8 qt. pressure cooker.* Cook for 45 to 50 minutes on medium. Always start counting after the pressure builds up and the temperature is lowered to medium.

*Once the meats are cooked, discard the bones from the ribs, shred the Tasajo meat, and transfer everything to a large stockpot and continue to cook over medium-high heat. Peel all the vegetables, and cut them into big chunks. Add the yuccas, 1 malanga, and the green plantain to the meats and broth in the stock pot. Add the rest of the seasonings, and taste. Add more salt if necessary. Bring to a boil, then reduce the heat to low, cover, and simmer for about 10 minutes. Add the 2 other malangas, ñame, and corn, and keep cooking for another 15 minutes. Add the yellow plantain, boniato, and calabaza; cook for 15 minutes more. Take out a few chunks of malangas and green plantains, and mash them outside the pot. Return them to the pot, add the "bollitos," and simmer, uncovered, for about 10 minutes more or until the soup thickens.

Note: Make the "bollitos" by cooking 1 cup of coarse cornmeal with 1½ cups of water, 1 tsp. of oil, and 1 tsp. of salt, until reduced and very thick (hard). Shape the nuggets with a spoon and place in the soup. If they separate, wait until they cool and get harder.

*Conventional Cooking Method
If not using a pressure cooker, place the 3 meats, onions, green bell pepper, garlic, cumin, and about 2 qts. of water in a large stockpot with a good lid, and bring to a boil. Reduce the heat, and cook for approximately 2 hours, or until all the meat is tender. Continue with the rest of the recipe from the second asterisk.

Seafood

Paella

Yellow Rice with Seafood/Chicken

Paella is another recipe from Spain that has been integrated into Cuban cuisine. This influence is evident in Cuban restaurants, which usually offer *paella* in their menus.

Serves 4 to 6

3 tbsp. olive oil
1 large onion, chopped
6 garlic cloves, mashed
1 red bell pepper, cut into thick slices
1 lb. boneless, skinless chicken, cut into big chunks
½ lb. ham, cut into cubes
1 chorizo cut into ½-inch slices
1 cup dry white wine
¼ tsp. cumin powder
Dash dried oregano leaves, crushed
Black pepper to taste
1 tbsp. salt
½ lb. shrimp, cleaned
2 lobster tails, cut into 3 sections
½ lb. crab claws
½ lb. scallops
¼ lb. squid, cut into rings
4 to 5 clams in their shells
5 to 6 oysters in their shells
½ lb. mussels in their shells
½ lb. fillet of fish in chunks
1 small can tomato paste (about 3 tbsp.)
1 can sweet red pimentos, sliced (7 oz.)
3½ cups parboiled long-grain rice
Generous pinch saffron
1 beer (not dark) 12 oz.
3 cups water
1 can asparagus for decoration
1 can sweat peas for decoration (8 oz.)

Heat the oil in a very large and deep pan with a cover. Add the onions, garlic, and red bell peppers, and sauté until the onions are transparent. Add the chicken, ham, and sausage. Continue to sauté for several minutes while turning; add the wine, cumin, oregano, black pepper, and salt. Cook the chicken for about 15 minutes or until it is golden. Add the seafood and the chunks of fish. Add the tomato paste and the sweet red pimentos with their liquid. Mix everything well. Add the rice and sauté for 1 minute, scraping the bottom to prevent sticking. Add the rest of the ingredients, except for the asparagus. Reduce the heat to low, cover the pan tightly, and simmer for about 20 minutes. If the rice still has too much liquid, uncover and simmer, allowing the excess liquid to evaporate. If it seems too dry, add more water or cooking wine.

Variation: Soupier Rice; *a la Chorrera*

For soupier rice (*a la chorrera*), use short-grain, Valencia style rice instead of parboiled rice; use 5½ cups of water, instead of 3; and use 2 beers, instead of 1. This recipe can also be cooked in a very large pressure cooker. After the pressure builds, reduce the heat to medium and cook for 15 minutes. Put the cooker in the sink, and let cool water run over the top until all the pressure is gone. Open and stir carefully. Serve at once.

Variation: Chicken Paella

Remove the seafood and fish from the above recipe, and add about 2 lbs. more chicken. Follow the above directions.

Note: Can use Polska or turkey Kielbasa if chorizo is unavailable. In Spain, they leave the shell on the shrimp. I peel them. Can use ½ tsp. red coloring in place of Saffron.

Seafood in Spanish Wine Sauce

Zarzuela de Mariscos

Zarzuela is a dish from Spain and is almost as popular as *Paella*. It is a delicious way to cook an array of seafood in a wonderful wine sauce.

Serves 6

4 tbsp. olive oil
1 onion, chopped (Vidalia onion is best)
6 large garlic cloves, mashed
3 lobster tails, cut into 3 sections each
½ lb. large scallops
½ lb. squid, cut in rings
2 or 3 clams in their shells
5 or 6 oysters in their shells
½ lb. mussels in their shells
½ lb. white fish-fillet, cut in chunks; use solid meat fish (optional)
½ cup Pinot Grigio wine or any dry white wine
1 tsp. salt
¼ tsp. cumin powder
Pinch dried oregano leaves, crushed
Black pepper to taste
½ can tomato paste (6 oz.)
1 lb. shrimp, peeled and cleaned
½ cup dry sherry or cognac for flaming

Heat oil in a deep, large skillet. Add onions and garlic, and sauté for about 1 minute. Add all the seafood except the shrimp and sauté, turning constantly. Add the white wine, salt, and other condiments. Check the taste, and add more salt and pepper if necessary. Add the tomato paste, and keep turning until the lobster tails are bright pink. Add the shrimp, and cook for 5 more minutes. In a separate skillet, heat the cognac or sherry. Remove from heat, and ignite it with a match or lighter. Let flames die away, and pour it on the seafood, turning it and letting it soak up the flavor. Serve at once

Yellow Rice with Seafood

Arroz con Mariscos a la Chorrera

This rice can also be made with only shrimp or a combination of shrimp and chicken breasts cut into small chunks. It is a very quick way to cook a delicious meal.

Serves 6

3 tbsp. olive oil
1 large onion, chopped
6 garlic cloves, mashed
1 lb. shrimp, peeled and cleaned
2 lobster tails, cut into 3 sections each
½ lb. scallops and/or squid, cut into rings
3 to 4 clams in their shells
5 to 6 oysters in their shells
½ lb. solid fish (such as grouper), cut into chunks
Black pepper to taste
¼ tsp. cumin powder
Pinch red pepper, crushed
2 tsp. salt
1 cup dry white wine
1 small can tomato paste (about 3 tbsp.)
1 can sweet red pimentos, sliced, with liquid (7 oz.)
1 small can *petit pois* or sweet peas (8 oz.)
3 cups Valencia-style rice (short grain)
1 beer (not dark) 12 oz.
5½ cups water
Generous pinch saffron (or ½ tsp. red coloring)
1 can white asparagus for decorating

Heat the oil in a large pressure cooker.* Add the onions, garlic, and sauté until the onions are transparent. Add the seafood and the fish. Continue to sauté for 2 minutes while turning; add all the spices and the salt. Add the white wine, tomato paste, sweet red pimentos (sliced) with its liquid, and the can of peas. Mix everything well. Add the rice, the beer, the water, and the red coloring or saffron. Turn some more. Check the taste, and add more salt if necessary. Cover the pressure cooker, wait for the pressure to build, and cook for 20 minutes over medium heat. After 20 minutes, take the cooker to the sink and let cool water run over the cooker until the pressure is gone; the vent valve will go down. Open the cooker and serve immediately. Rice will be soupy, which is called *a la chorrera*. Decorate with white asparagus.

*Conventional Cooking Method

Use a 5 to 6 qt. Dutch oven or large, deep skillet fitted with a good lid. Start sautéing on medium/high heat. After adding the rice and liquids, bring to a boil. Reduce heat to low and cook for about 30 minutes. Rice will be soupy or *a la chorrera*.

Shrimp and Lobster Enchilado (in Spicy Tomato Sauce)

Camarones y Langosta Enchilados

This delicious recipe was the signature dish served on the famous Cuban beaches. Because it is an island, Cuba is surrounded by beautiful beaches where restaurants took pride in serving the freshest and most succulent seafood, especially shrimp.

Serves 4 to 6

1 onion (Vidalia or yellow), minced
6 large garlic cloves, mashed
½ red or green bell pepper
1 can sweet red pimentos (7 oz.)
¼ cup olive oil
1 can tomato puree or paste (6 oz.)
1 tsp. salt
¼ tsp. black pepper
Pinch crushed red pepper
A dash Tabasco hot sauce (optional)
¼ tsp. cumin powder
¾ cup dry white wine
2 lbs. peeled and cleaned shrimp, or lobster tails cut in sections or both
¼ cup sherry

Sauce can be prepared ahead of time. Sauté the onions, garlic, peppers, and pimentos in olive oil in a large skillet for 2 or 3 minutes. Add the tomato puree, salt, pepper, red pepper, Tabasco if desired, cumin, and white wine. Simmer over low heat for 15 to 20 minutes. If prepared ahead of time, turn off the heat until time to eat. Ten minutes before dinner time, add shrimps and/or lobster, add sherry, and cook for 5 to 7 minutes. Shrimps should not be cooked longer or they will become hard and chewy. Serve immediately over white rice.

Note: You can add a combination of seafood such as scallops, shrimps, lobster, clams, and boneless fish to this recipe for a wonderful seafood feast.

Garlic Shrimp

Camarones al Ajillo

This is the easiest and fastest recipe in this cookbook. I always recommend it to the inexperienced cook.

Serves 4

¼ cup olive oil
8 large garlic cloves, mashed
2 lbs. fresh shrimp, peeled and cleaned
Dash dry oregano leaves, crushed
Black pepper and salt to taste

In a large, deep skillet, heat olive oil and add the garlic. Sauté a little, and add shrimp, oregano, and a good sprinkle of freshly ground black pepper and salt. Sauté until the shrimp are pink, about 5 minutes, turning often. Serve immediately.

Variation: Garlic Shrimp with Mushrooms

For a different taste, sauté about ½ cup of sliced Portabella mushrooms with the garlic cloves. After adding the shrimp, add ½ cup of dry sherry, and cook for 5 minutes.

Rice with Squid

Arroz con Calamares

The squid used in this recipe is the canned variety, which is packed in its own ink. This is what will give the dark-gray color to the rice.

Serves 2 to 4

2 tbsp. olive oil
1 medium onion, chopped
½ green bell pepper, chopped
5 garlic cloves, mashed
Dash cumin powder
2 cans squid chunks, in its ink (Spanish section of the super-market; 4 to 5 oz. cans)
1 cup long-grain rice
¼ cup cooking wine
1 tsp. salt
1½ cups water

Heat oil in a 2 qt. sauce pan. Add onions, green pepper, garlic, cumin, and squid with its liquid/oil. Sauté for about 2 minutes, turning often. Add the rice, wine, salt, and water. Bring to a boil and cook for about 1 minute, turning to prevent sticking. Cover and reduce heat to low. Cook for 20 minutes. Flake with a fork before serving.

Vizcayan-Style Cod Fish

Bacalao a la Vizcaina

This recipe was brought to Cuba by a large population of Spaniards from Vizcaya, the Northern coast of Spain, where fresh fish abounds.

Serves 4 to 6

2 lbs. dry, salted cod fish, boneless and skinless
2 medium potatoes, peeled and cut into ½-inch slices
¼ cup olive oil
1 medium onion (Vidalia or yellow), minced
6 large garlic cloves, mashed
½ red or green bell pepper
1 can sweet red pimentos (7 oz.)
¼ tsp. cumin powder
Dash oregano
¼ tsp. black pepper
½ cup dry white wine
1 can tomato puree or paste (6 oz.)
Dash Tabasco hot sauce (optional)
3 to 4 tbsp. vinegar
Pimento stuffed olives to garnish
1 can sweat peas to garnish (8 oz.)

Soak the cod fish in water for about 15 minutes. Discard the water and pour more fresh water, soaking the fish for about 1 more hour. Drain and discard the water. Put fresh water in a pot, and boil the cod fish over medium heat until tender, about 30 minutes. Drain the fish and reserve, but do not discard water. In the same water, boil the potatoes until they are almost cooked—they should be firm.

In a large, deep skillet, heat the oil and sauté the onions, garlic, bell peppers, and red pimentos, stirring constantly, for about 1 minute. Add the cod fish and sauté while adding the rest of the ingredients except the vinegar. Stir everything. Add the potato slices, arranging them carefully around the skillet. Reduce the heat, cover, and simmer for approximately 20 minutes. Add the vinegar; you can add more wine if sauce begins to dry. Turn occasionally to prevent sticking; when turning the potatoes, be careful not to mash them. If not serving the cod fish right away, remove from heat and leave in the skillet until it is time to eat. Reheat over low heat for a few minutes. This extra time in the sauce enhances the flavor. Add the olives and peas as a garnish, if desired, when ready to serve. Olives add too much salt if added too soon. Serve with white rice.

Cod Fish and Potato Salad

Ensalada de Bacalao y Papas

Serves 4

1 lb. dry cod fish, boneless and skinless
2 medium potatoes, peeled and cut into ½-inch slices
½ cabbage, cut into chunks
1 medium white onion, sliced
4 to 5 tbsp. olive oil
3 to 4 tbsp. vinegar

Soak the cod fish in water for about 15 minutes. Discard the water, pour more fresh water, and soak fish for 1 hour. Drain and discard the water. Pour fresh water in a pot, add the cod fish, and bring to a boil. Reduce the heat to medium, and cook for 30 minutes or until tender. Drain the fish and reserve the water in the pot. Transfer the fish to a large salad bowl, and flake-apart the meat with a fork. In the reserved water, boil the potatoes and the cabbage until cooked, about 15 minutes; they should be firm, not mushy. Drain the potatoes and the cabbage, and transfer to the salad bowl. Mix them well with the cod fish, and add the onion slices. Pour the olive oil on top of the salad, and sprinkle salad with the vinegar. Toss to mix. Serve hot or cold.

Grilled Salmon in Garlic Butter

Salmon a la Parrilla

Serves 4 to 6

2 lbs. salmon fillet with skin on
   1 side
Salt and pepper to taste
2 tbsp. butter
5 large garlic cloves, mashed
Aluminum foil to cook

Cut salmon fillet into 4 sections; use kitchen scissors to cut through the skin. Sprinkle with salt and black pepper. In the microwave, melt the butter with the mashed garlic in a small bowl, about 1 minute. Brush the salmon meat with the garlic butter. Heat a BBQ grill and reduce the heat to low. Cut 4 strips of aluminum foil about 6 x 12 inches each. Place 1 piece of salmon fillet, skin side down, on top of one half of one of the foil pieces, and fold over the other half of the foil. Do not let it touch the meat. It should be loosely folded over the meat. Do the same with the other 3 pieces of salmon. Grill over low heat for about 12 minutes, or until the salmon is cooked completely. Try flaking the widest part to see if the meat is cooked inside.

Variation: Grilled Mahi-Mahi
   Delfin a la Parrilla
Follow the instructions above, replacing the salmon with mahi-mahi.

Dijon Salmon with Sliced Potatoes

Salmon con Ruedas de Papas

Serves 4 to 6

½ cup Dijon mustard
½ cup vegetable oil
½ cup dill weed
5 tbsp brown sugar
2 lbs. salmon
3 baking potatoes

Mix the first 4 ingredients in a bowl, cover with foil, and allow it to sit for an hour. Preheat oven to 400 degrees. Place salmon in oven pan. Slice the potatoes into ¼-inch slices. Boil them until almost tender. Spread sauce over salmon. Surround the salmon with the potato slices. Bake in oven for 20 minutes. Serve immediately.

Chicken and Turkey

Arroz con Pollo

Yellow Rice with Chicken

Everyone knows *Arroz con Pollo*, because it is the best known of all Cuban recipes, although some might argue that title goes to Black Beans. To me, *Arroz con Pollo* is the fastest way to cook a complete, delicious meal in 30 minutes if you use a pressure cooker, or 1 hour if you don't. My favorite way of cooking this recipe is the variation at the bottom of the regular recipe: *a la Chorrera*.

Serves 4 to 6

3 tbsp. olive oil
¼ lb. cooking ham, cut into small cubes
1 medium onion, chopped
5 or 6 large garlic cloves, mashed
2 lbs. chicken, cut into pieces (thighs, breasts, drumsticks, etc.)
Pinch saffron or ½ tsp. yellow coloring
¼ tsp. cumin powder
1½ tsp. salt
Dash black pepper
Dash dry oregano
½ cup white wine or cooking wine
1 can sweet red pimentos (7 oz.)
1 small can *petit pois* or sweet peas (8 oz.)
1 small can corn (optional; 8 oz.)
½ can tomato paste (6 oz.)
2½ cups long-grain rice or par-boiled rice
12 oz. beer (not dark)
1½ cup water
Pimento-stuffed olives (optional)

Heat the oil in a pressure cooker.* Add the ham, the onions, and the garlic. Sauté for about 1 minute, turning constantly. Add the chicken, and sauté while adding the spices.

Add the wine; the can of red pimentos, sliced, with the liquid too; the sweet peas; the corn, if desired; and the tomato paste, turning after every addition. Add the rice, mixing it with the other ingredients. Add the beer, the water, and the coloring.

*Close the pressure cooker, and wait until the pressure indicator or vent says there is pressure. Reduce the heat to medium, and cook for 25 minutes. When the pressure is gone, open the cooker and fluff the rice with a cooking fork.

Variation: *A la Chorrera*

For soupy rice, *a la Chorrera*, use short-grain Valencia-style rice, and use 3½ cups of water instead of 1. The rest of the ingredients should remain the same. When the cooking time is up, take the pressure cooker to the sink and let cool water run over the cooker until the pressure is gone. Open at once, stir the rice carefully, and serve immediately.

*Conventional Cooking Method

Heat the oil in a large Dutch oven or stockpot. Continue with the recipe up to the second asterisk. After sautéing all the ingredients, as indicated, add 1 extra cup of water. Bring to a boil, turning constantly, and then reduce the heat to medium-low. Cover with a tight-fitting lid, and cook for approximately 45 minutes, stirring occasionally and scraping the bottom. If using the *a la Chorrera* variation, add more liquid (beer, wine, or water) during the cooking process as necessary, to keep the rice soupy.

Imperial Rice

Arroz Imperial

Imperial Rice is a very elegant way of serving chicken with rice. It is very popular for parties, because it yields more rice and the chicken is shredded, instead of served in large pieces as it is with traditional *arroz con pollo*. This recipe is the best you will find, because the chicken meat is cooked in the very flavorful sauce after is has been shredded.

Serves 4 to 6

2 lbs. chicken breasts
1 tbsp. salt
2 Vidalia or yellow onions
¼ green bell pepper
3 tbsp. olive oil
5 or 6 large garlic cloves, mashed
1 small can tomato paste (6 oz.)
¼ cup cooking wine or dry white wine
10 to 12 pimento-stuffed olives
¼ tsp. cumin powder
Dash dry oregano
Salt and black pepper to taste
1 can sweet red pimentos with liquid (7 oz.)
5 cups chicken broth
12 oz. beer (regular, not dark)
2 cups Valencia-style rice (short grain)
Saffron, to color the rice
Mayonnaise (used when serving)

Boil the chicken until fully cooked and tender, in 6 cups of water with salt; 1 onion, cut into 4 chunks; and the green bell pepper. Let cool, and shred with your hands or 2 forks. Reserve the broth.

In a deep, large skillet, heat the oil. Add 1 onion, finely chopped, and the garlic cloves. Sauté for about 1 minute. Add the chicken, ¾ can of the tomato paste, wine, olives, and spices. Sauté, turning constantly. Add sweet red pimentos cut into large slices; reserve some for the rice. Add 1 cup of the chicken broth, cover, and simmer over low heat for about 20 minutes. Add more broth if it begins to dry.

About 20 minutes before dinner time, heat 4½ cups of the chicken broth in the pressure cooker.* Add the beer, the rice, slices of sweet red pimentos, the remaining tomato paste, and enough saffron to give the broth an orange/yellow color. Add more salt if necessary.

*Close the pressure cooker, wait for the pressure to build, reduce the heat to medium, and cook for 17 minutes. Then put the cooker in the sink and pour cool water over it until the pressure is gone and it is safe to open. Open at once, and serve the rice in a large, rectangular, glass pan. It will be soupy. Serve the chicken over the rice. Spread mayonnaise over the chicken or serve on the side.

Variation: Party Presentation
Serve half of the rice in the rectangular glass dish, layer the chicken on top of the rice, and cover with the rest of the rice. Spread mayonnaise on top. It can be kept in the oven until serving. You can also top the dish with slices of ham and mozzarella cheese instead of mayonnaise. Heat until the cheese melts.

*Conventional Cooking Method
Use a large Dutch oven or stockpot, and continue with the recipe up to the second asterisk. Close the pot with a tight-fitting lid. Reduce the heat to medium-low, and cook for 30 minutes, stirring occasionally. If necessary, add more liquid while cooking, to keep the rice soupy. Follow the recipe's serving guide, or the party presentation variation.

Special Chicken Pie

Pastelon Camagueyano de Pollo

This recipe is my family's favorite! It is also the one recipe that brings the most beautiful memories of my childhood in Cuba. Everyone who has tried this pie absolutely *loves* it.

Yields 1 9-inch pie

Crust
2 cups all purpose flour
3 tbsp. sugar
1 tsp. salt
¾ cup vegetable shortening (Crisco)
1 tbsp. rum or whiskey
4 to 5 tbsp. water
1 egg, beaten

Pie Filling
4 chicken breast halves
½ onion
¼ green pepper
1 tbsp. salt
4 tbsp. olive oil
1 medium onion, finely chopped
5 or 6 large garlic cloves, mashed or minced
1 can red pimentos, sliced (7 oz.)
⅓ cup dry white wine (or cooking wine)
½ can tomato puree or paste (6 oz. can)
¼ tsp. cumin powder
10 to 12 pimento stuffed olives
½ tsp. salt
Pinch black pepper

To prepare the **Crust,** mix all the dry ingredients together first. Add the shortening, and mix in the mixer with dough blades or mix by hand. Add the rum and the water until the dough forms a ball. If dough gets too sticky, sprinkle it with more flour. Separate the dough into 2 balls. Using a rolling pin, roll out each one to form a circle. Stretch the dough to the size of the pie dish, plus 1 more inch.

To avoid dough sticking to the rolling pin or countertop, use a piece of wax paper or plastic sheet above and below the dough when rolling it out.

To prepare the **Pie Filling,** boil the chicken until tender in 4 cups of water with onion, green pepper, and salt. Let cool. Shred the chicken by hand or with 2 forks.

Heat oil in large, deep skillet, and sauté the onions, garlic, and red pimentos for about 1 minute. Add the chicken, the dry white wine, the tomato paste or puree, the rest of the spices, and the olives. Check the taste, and add more salt if necessary. Simmer over medium-low heat, turning constantly to avoid burning the bottom. When most of the liquid has evaporated, the mixture is ready to be added to the pie. If the chicken has too much liquid, it will make the bottom crust soggy.

Place one of the dough circles in the pie dish; it must cover the entire bottom and sides. Fill with chicken mixture, and cover with the other circle of pie dough. Pinch the sides together with a fork or fingers. Brush the pie top with the beaten egg and cut a few slits on the top crust. Bake at 350 degrees for 20 to 25 minutes or until golden in color.

Variation: Alternate Filling

Try a different filling such as tuna, instead of chicken, in the above recipe, or ham and Swiss cheese.

Chicken Fricassee (Chicken in Spicy Tomato Sauce)

Fricase de Pollo

Serves 4

3 tbsp. olive oil
1 medium onion, chopped
5 to 6 large garlic cloves, mashed
¼ red or green bell pepper, chopped
2 lb. chicken, cut up or 2 lbs. chicken legs or thighs
¼ cup Marsala wine or sherry
½ cup red wine
½ can tomato puree or paste (6 oz. can)
1 large potato, peeled and cut in chunks
1 can sweet red pimentos (7 oz.)
¼ tsp. cumin powder
Dash dry oregano (This is strong, so use according to taste preference)
1 tsp. salt
Dash black pepper
Pimento-stuffed olives (about 10)
Handful raisins (optional)

Heat the oil in a pressure cooker.* Add the onion, garlic, and red or green bell pepper. Sauté for about 1 minute, turning constantly. Add the chicken pieces, and sauté while adding the wine, tomato puree or paste, and the rest of the ingredients. Be sure to add the liquid from the pimento can and cut the pimentos into slices. Check the taste, and add more salt if necessary.

*Cover the cooker. When the valve indicates there is pressure, turn the heat down to medium, and cook for 25 minutes. Serve with white rice.

*Conventional Cooking Method

Use a large Dutch oven or stockpot, and follow the above recipe up to the second asterisk. Cover the pot with a tight-fitting lid, add 1 cup of water, and cook on medium heat for 1 hour or until the meat is tender.

Chicken or Turkey Pot Pie
Pastel de Pollo en Caserola

You can also make this with a sweeter crust by adding more sugar, or a saltier crust by adding more salt.

Serves 6 to 8

Pie Filling
2½ lbs. of boneless, skinless chicken breasts (or turkey), cut into cubes
2 garlic cloves, mashed
1 onion, chopped
2 tsp. salt
¼ green bell pepper
1 potato, cut up into small cubes
2 carrots, cut into ¼-inch slices
1 cup frozen green peas (*petit pois*)
1 small can kernel corn, drained
2 celery stalks, cut into small slices
Dash cumin powder
Dash black pepper
3 tbsp. butter
2 tbsp. flour

Crust
2⅔ cups all purpose flour
2 tbsp. sugar
1 tsp. salt
1 cup butter or vegetable shortening
1 tbsp. rum or whiskey
5 to 6 tbsp. water
1 egg, beaten (for glazing the pie)
9" x 13" glass baking dish

To prepare the **Pie Filling,** boil the chicken breasts in 4 to 6 cups of water, with the garlic, ½ the onion, salt, and the bell pepper until the meat is tender, about 20 minutes. Afterwards, add all the vegetables and the spices. Simmer for several minutes until the potatoes are tender but firm. Keep the pot uncovered to help evaporate some of the liquid. In a small sauce pot, melt the butter and add the flour, turning quickly to form a ball. Add some of the broth from the chicken (about ½ cup) and keep turning to smooth the sauce. Pour the flour and butter sauce into the pot with the chicken and vegetables; stir carefully to smooth out any lumps without mashing the potatoes. Simmer for a couple more minutes and remove from the heat. Transfer to a 9" by 13" glass baking dish. Do not fill up to the top with the chicken and vegetable mixture or the dish will overflow in the oven.

To prepare the **Crust,** mix all the dry ingredients for the crust in a large bowl. Add the butter, and mix together completely. Add the rum and 3 tablespoons of water. Knead with hands, adding the rest of the water until dough separates from the sides of the bowl. If dough is too sticky, sprinkle it with more flour. If dough crumbles too much, sprinkle it with more water. Make 1 ball with the dough.

On a clean countertop, place a large sheet of plastic wrap. Place the dough in the center of the plastic wrap, cover with another sheet of plastic wrap, and flatten it with a rolling pin to form a rectangle 1-inch wider and longer than the glass baking dish you are using to bake the pie. Crust should be a little thick, about ¼-inch-thick, because you are not using one for the bottom. Take off the top plastic wrap, and place the baking dish next to the crust. Holding the crust with the bottom plastic wrap, transfer the crust to the glass baking dish where the chicken pot pie is. Cover completely with the crust, and press the edges over the rim of the pan to seal. Cut several slits on top of the crust with a sharp knife. Brush the crust with the beaten egg. Bake in a 350 degree oven for 25 minutes, or until the crust is golden brown.

Chicken with Pasta

Pasta con Pollo

This pasta dish is very convenient, because the pasta is cooked together with the chicken. There is no need to boil it separately.

Serves 6

4 chicken breasts, boneless and skinless
3 tbsp. olive or cooking oil
1 large onion, chopped
6 large garlic cloves, mashed
½ green bell pepper, chopped
1 can tomato paste (6 oz.)
1 can crushed tomatoes (15 oz.)
¼ cup red wine
¼ cup Marsala wine
1½ tsp. salt
⅛ tsp. black pepper
¼ tsp. cumin powder
¼ tsp. dried oregano leaves, crushed
1 box mostaccioli rigati pasta or ziti (16 oz.)
1 bag shredded or grated Parmesan cheese (14 oz.) (Best choice: Reggiano Parmesan)

Cut chicken breasts into small chunks, about 1-inch pieces. Heat oil in the pressure cooker.* Add onions, garlic, and green bell pepper, and sauté for 1 minute. Add chicken, and sauté while adding tomato paste, crushed tomatoes, wines, and spices.

Add 1 cup of water, close the cooker, and turn down the heat to medium after the pressure builds. Cook for 20 minutes. When the pressure is gone, open the cooker.

Add 1 cup of water to the chicken, and add the uncooked pasta. Cook pasta over medium heat, turning often to avoid sticking. After 10 minutes, add the parmesan cheese and cook for another 2 to 3 minutes. This recipe should be saucy. Adjust the sauce by adding more wine or water while the pasta is cooking.

*Conventional Cooking Method

Use a large Dutch oven or stockpot, and sauté the chicken, vegetables, and spices as above. Then, cover the pot with a tight-fitting lid, add 1½ cups of water, and cook over medium heat for 45 minutes, or until the chicken is tender. Continue the above recipe from the addition of the pasta and water.

Chunky Chicken Salad

Ensalada de Pollo Crujiente

This salad is perfect for a low fat, high protein diet, and it is delicious!

Serves 6

4 chicken breast halves
2 apples, cored and cut into cubes
½ cup chopped onions or green onions
2 large celery stalks, chopped
2 eggs, boiled and chopped
½ cup mayonnaise (light or regular)
Salt and pepper to taste
½ cup sliced almonds

Boil chicken breasts in salted water for about 30 minutes, or until completely cooked. Add a piece of onion and green pepper to add flavor if desired. Let cool and shred the chicken with your hands or with two forks. Combine all the ingredients, except for the almonds, in a large bowl. Spread the chicken salad into a 9" x 13" glass pan. Toast the almonds by spreading them in a single layer on a baking sheet and broiling for approximately 2 minutes, checking constantly that they do not burn. Sprinkle the almonds on top of the salad. Serve salad chilled with dinner rolls or crackers.

Chicken Pot Roast

Pollo Asado en la Olla

Serves 4

1 whole chicken, cut up into quarts or 2 lbs. chicken quarts
1 cup juice from sour oranges
6 garlic cloves, mashed
1 tsp. salt
Dash black pepper
¼ tsp. dry oregano
¼ tsp. cumin powder
4 tbsp. olive oil
1 medium onion, sliced
½ cup cooking wine or dry white wine

Marinate the chicken for a few hours or overnight with ½ cup of the sour orange juice, 2 garlic cloves, salt, black pepper, oregano, and cumin powder. Rub the chicken on all sides with all the ingredients. Cover with plastic wrap, and keep in the refrigerator until time to cook.

Heat the oil in a pressure cooker,* while adding the chicken. Brown the chicken on all sides. Add the onions, the rest of the garlic, the remaining juice from the sour oranges, and the wine. Add all the juices from the marinade as well.

Close the pressure cooker, and wait for the pressure to build. Reduce the heat to medium, and cook for 25 minutes. Wait for the pressure to subside completely. Open the cooker and check the liquid. Turn the heat back on and, being careful not to burn the chicken, reduce the liquid to a thicker sauce. Place the chicken on a serving dish, and pour the cooking juices over it.

*Conventional Cooking Method
Heat the oil in a large Dutch oven or stockpot. Brown the chicken and add the ingredients as directed above. Then, add 1 cup of water and close the pot. Reduce the heat to medium, and cook for 1 hour or until the chicken is tender. Open the pot during the last 10 minutes of cooking to allow the excess liquid to evaporate, to thicken the sauce.

Fried Chicken Cuban Style

Pollo Frito Estilo Cubano

Serves 4

2 lbs. chicken legs and/or thighs, skin-on
5 or 6 large garlic cloves, mashed
Juice from 1 sour orange
Dash cumin powder
Salt and black pepper to taste
Cooking oil
½ cup lime juice
¼ cup onion, thinly sliced

A few hours before cooking, rub the chicken with half the garlic cloves and the juice from the sour orange. Season with the cumin powder, salt, and pepper. Keep refrigerated until ready to cook.

In a deep fryer, heat the oil and place the chicken pieces in it. Brown the chicken on all sides. Reduce the heat to medium, and fry until the chicken is cooked and crispy. Remove from oil and place on paper towels to drain. Transfer to a serving plate. Mix the rest of the mashed garlic cloves with the lime juice, and pour on the meat. Garnish with the onion slices, and serve.

Mexican Enchiladas

Enchiladas Mejicanas

Serves 6

3 tbsp. olive oil
1 medium onion, finely chopped
3 green onions, chopped
½ green bell pepper, finely chopped
4 chicken breasts, boiled and shredded
½ can tomato puree or paste
¼ tsp. cumin powder
¼ tsp. dried oregano leaves
Salt and black pepper to taste
2 cups sour cream
1 bag (16 oz.) shredded Mexican cheeses (Monterey Jack, etc.)
3 coriander (cilantro) leaves, chopped
2 cups Mexican Salsa (Pico de Gallo), hot or mild
12 corn tortillas

Heat oil in deep skillet, and add the onions and bell peppers. Sauté for about 1 minute. Add the chicken, tomato puree or paste, the spices, and the salt and pepper. Sauté, mixing everything together and turning constantly. Remove from heat, and transfer to a large bowl. Add 1 cup of the sour cream, 1 cup of the Mexican cheese, coriander leaves, and ½ cup of the Mexican salsa. Mix well.

Grease a rectangular 9" by 13" glass pan. Fill each corn tortilla with about 3 tbsp. of the chicken mixture. Roll up carefully, and place tortilla in the glass pan with the seam down. When you are done with this process, pour the rest of the Mexican salsa on top of the tortillas. Cover the pan with aluminum foil, and bake for 30 minutes in a 325 degree oven. After 30 minutes, uncover the dish, and sprinkle the rest of the Mexican cheese (1 cup) on top. Return to the oven and bake, uncovered, for another 7 minutes, or until the cheese melts. Remove pan from the oven, and pour the other cup of sour cream on top of the tortillas in a wide line at the center. Do this when you are ready to serve the dish.

Note: To avoid breaking the corn tortillas when rolling them, follow the instructions on the package.

Mexican Lasagna

Tortillas Mejicanas en Capas

Serves 8 to 10

3 tbsp. olive oil

1 onion, chopped

5 large garlic cloves, mashed

¼ red and green bell peppers, chopped

4 chicken breasts, cubed

½ cup cooking or dry white wine

2 jars (about 2 cups) chunky salsa, medium or hot

Salt and black pepper to taste

10 large, Mexican-style flour tortillas

2 lbs. shredded four Mexican cheeses

1 cup sour cream

Heat the oil in a medium sauce pot, and add the onion, garlic, and bell peppers. Sauté for 1 minute, turning constantly. Add the chicken pieces, and sauté while adding the wine, 1 cup of salsa, and the spices. Cover and simmer over medium-low heat for about 20 minutes, or until the chicken is tender. Uncover and simmer for a few minutes until the excess liquid evaporates. Grease the bottom of a rectangular glass pan and arrange the tortillas to cover the bottom and sides. Spread a layer of the chicken over the tortillas, then add a layer of the shredded cheese. Repeat the process until you have used up all of the chicken. Top with a layer of tortilla, 1 cup of salsa, and cheese. Bake in 350 degree oven until the cheese melts. Serve with sour cream.

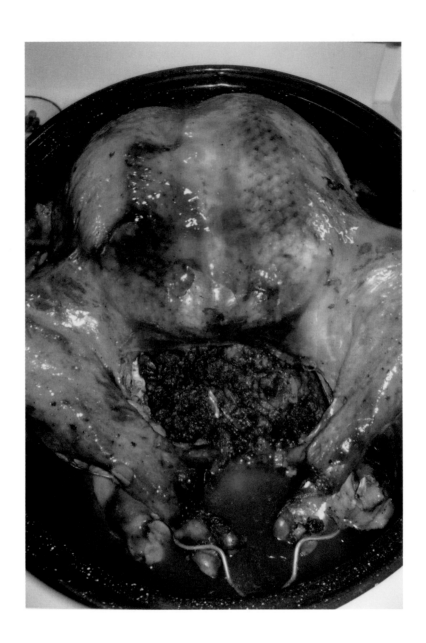

Roasted, Stuffed Turkey

Pavo Relleno Asado

Turkey
1 turkey (15 to 22 lbs.)
1 cup red wine

Mojo
1 cup juice from sour oranges or ½
    cup vinegar and ½ cup lime juice
5 or 6 garlic cloves, mashed
1 tsp. salt
¼ tsp. cumin powder
¼ tsp. dried oregano leaves, crushed
⅛ tsp. black pepper

Cuban Stuffing
6 slices bacon, cut into 1-inch
    pieces
1 large onion, finely chopped
1 Spanish sausage, skin peeled off
½ lb. ground ham
½ lb. ground pork
½ lb. ground beef (optional)
¼ cup Marsala wine or dry sherry
¾ cup raisins, prunes, or dates
¾ cups chopped walnuts
¼ cup sliced almonds
1 apple, cored and cubed
1 tbsp. tomato paste
½ cup red wine
1 tsp. salt
¼ tsp. cumin powder
¼ tsp. dried oregano leaves, crushed
⅛ tsp. black pepper
3½ cups dry cornbread stuffing

To prepare the **Turkey,** the night before you plan to cook the turkey, inject the turkey with the cup of red wine using a syringe with a thick needle. These are sold in stores where kitchen utensils are sold. Insert the needle in all the meaty parts of the turkey.

To prepare the **Mojo,** mix all ingredients together.

Pour the mojo over the turkey and spread it all over and into the cavity. I do not advise cutting slits into the meat to put the mojo in, because that step might let the natural juices escape during roasting.

To prepare the **Cuban Stuffing,** cook the slices of bacon over medium heat in a large, deep skillet until almost crunchy. Add the onion, the sausage, and all the ground meats. Cook, breaking apart the lumps of meat, and turning constantly. Add the wine, and the rest of the ingredients except for the cornbread stuffing. Cook for a few minutes until the meat is done, and turn off the heat. In a large bowl, prepare half of the cornmeal stuffing, and mix it into the meat stuffing. This stuffing is only used to keep the ingredients together. In traditional Cuban cooking, the cornmeal is not used.

Fill the turkey cavities with the stuffing, sewing the skin to prevent the stuffing from spilling out. Roast in a large, covered Dutch oven at 250 degrees for approximately 5 to 6 hours.

Note: If you prefer roasting the turkey in a regular roasting pan, cover the turkey with aluminum foil, and check after 6 hours. The cooking time for this method is longer. When the meat is almost done, remove the foil, and let the skin get more direct heat for a more appealing color.

Optional Glaze: To give the turkey a beautiful golden color, make a heavy syrup by boiling ½ cup of maple syrup with 2 to 3 tbsp. of brown sugar for a couple of minutes. Brush the syrup all over the turkey approximately 30 minutes before removing it from the oven and keep it uncovered during the last 30 minutes.

Turkey Fricassee
Fricase de Pavo

For Cubans, Turkey Fricassee is traditionally served during the Christmas Eve dinner, alongside the roast pork.

Serves 10

12 to 15 lbs. turkey, cut up in sections (or trays of breasts and thighs)
1 cup juice from sour oranges
8 large garlic cloves, mashed
½ tsp. cumin powder
½ tsp. dry oregano leaves, crushed
Salt and black pepper to taste
3 tbsp. olive oil
1 large onion, chopped
½ red or green bell pepper, chopped
2 cups red wine
½ cup Marsala or sherry wine
1 can tomato puree or paste
1 can sweet red pimentos, sliced (add the liquid also)
12 pimento-stuffed olives
¾ cup raisins (optional)

The night before cooking the turkey, cut it into smaller pieces. If buying the trays with whole breasts and thighs (wings are also good), cut them into 2 or 3 pieces each. If buying a whole turkey, cut it up into manageable sections, and cut the breast meat into chunks. Season the turkey with the sour orange juice, ½ of the mashed garlic, cumin powder, oregano, salt, and black pepper. Cover with plastic wrap and refrigerate to marinate overnight.

Heat the oil in a 6 qt. or larger pressure cooker.* Add the onion, the rest of the garlic, and the red or green bell pepper. Sauté for about 1 minute, turning constantly. Add the turkey with the marinade, and sauté while adding the wine, tomato puree or paste, and the rest of the ingredients. Check the taste, and add more salt if necessary.

Cover the cooker and wait for the pressure to build. Reduce the heat to medium, and cook for 40 minutes. After it is safe to open the cooker, check the turkey for tenderness. Simmer, uncovered, for a few minutes to thicken the sauce if needed.

*Conventional Cooking Method
Use an 8 qt. or larger stockpot, and add and sauté all the ingredients as above. Cover the pot with a tight-fitting lid, add 1 cup of water, and cook over medium heat for 1½ hours or until the meat is tender.

Pork, Beef, and Other Meats

Roast Pig, Cuban Style

Lechon Asado

The pig is the star of the Cuban *Nochebuena*, or Christmas Eve. For Cubans, Christmas Eve is an all day event. Family members start coming early in the morning to help place the pig in the roaster of choice. After that, neighbors and friends join them to "check" on the progress of the cooking, while drinking beer and eating fried pork skins.

Roasted Pig
A 50 lb. to 80 lb. pig, fresh or
    frozen

Mojo
4 cups juice from sour oranges or
    1 part orange juice to 3 parts
    lime juice
1 cup white vinegar
1 cup lime juice
15 to 18 large garlic cloves,
    mashed
1 tbsp. cumin powder
1 tbsp. dry oregano leaves,
    crushed
2 to 3 tbsp. salt
1 tbsp. black pepper

Important note: The pig must be bought gutted, cleaned, and perfectly shaved. Frozen pigs already are prepared this way. The night before roasting it, the pig must be thawed if it is a frozen pig, or it must be kept cool if fresh. Plan accordingly. When buying a fresh pig, bring it home the day before, and keep it cool with bags of ice or place it in a horizontal freezer for a couple of hours. Do not allow it to stay warm. If buying the pig frozen, take it out of the box early in the morning to give it enough time to thaw. Wash completely with a hose (outside, of course!) and dry with paper towels. Place on a large pan, skin up, and place the pan on a table or countertop to prepare it for cooking the next day.

Preparing the Pig

The evening before the pig roast, salt the entire skin of the pig and place the pig skin-side-down on a clean, sturdy surface. With a heavy knife or ax and hammer, cut through the side of the neck, the top of the backbone, and some top ribs. You will need to split the pig, so cut enough that you can press the pig open. Place your hands on both upper legs, and push down on them until the backbone cracks open. Now that the pig is completely split open, slit a few tiny holes into the meat with a thin, sharp knife. Especially make cuts in the 2 shoulders, the 2 hams (back legs), and the meat alongside the backbone.

Prepare the **Mojo** by blending all the ingredients together.

Pour the Mojo liberally on the entire inside of the pig, stuffing it in the tiny holes you made. Rub the Mojo on the rest of the legs, ribcage, neck, and even the head. Be generous with the amount you pour. Salt the feet to avoid smells, and cover the pig with plastic wrap or aluminum foil. Leave the pig inside the house overnight with a cool temperature. If in doubt, put ice cubes in zippered freezer bags, and place the bags on top of the covered pig. The leftover Mojo is used later to brush the pig or to spoon on the meat when served.

Roasting the Pig

The pig should be roasted in a BBQ or homemade pig roaster large enough that the charcoal will be at least 18 inches away from the meat. Secure the pig on 2 steel frames, 1 on top and 1 on the bottom, secured with wires on the sides to press the pig between the two. You can make these frames by welding ¼-inch rods together in a window-pane pattern. This will allow you to turn the pig easily when cooking and checking on it. This 2-frame set-up is optional and easier, but you don't have to have it on a separate rack.

Pile a good amount of charcoal, about 1 bucket, and light. When all coals are lit, separate the charcoal into 4 piles, and place the piles on the 4 corners of the charcoal rack of the roaster. The piles will be under the four feet of the pig. This will give an indirect heat to roast the pig and will prevent any flames from falling grease from burning any of the meat. Place the pig, already in the wire racks, skin up on the top rack of the BBQ, and close the lid. If there is no lid, cover with heavy aluminum foil. Every ½ hour, add 5 to 6 charcoals to every pile. This will keep a steady, low temperature, which is ideal for the pig to cook slowly and completely.

The cooking time varies depending on the type of roaster. We use a special homemade pig BBQ (my husband is a welder), with sliding doors in the front and back to add the charcoal easily. Because it has a good lid, the cooking time is approximately 8 hours for a 60 lb. pig. The Chinese Box roaster, used by many Cubans in Miami, cooks the pig in less time but the pig will not have a smoked flavor.

The pig is cooked if melted grease comes out when you poke the pig with a fork through the skin. Carefully turn the pig over, lifting it by two legs, and check the meat for tenderness. If you want the skin to be crispier, turn the pig on its back. Add more charcoal to the piles, and, when completely lit, spread the charcoal to cover the bottom rack. This process should broil the skin to make it crispy. Transfer the cooked pig to a serving table, and remove from the wires to serve. Add the leftover Mojo when serving the meat.

Pork Fricassee (Pork in Spicy Tomato Sauce)
Fricase de Puerco

Serves 4

3 tbsp. cooking oil
1 medium onion, chopped
5 to 6 large garlic cloves, mashed
½ green bell pepper, chopped
½ red bell pepper, chopped
2 lbs. lean pork meat, cut into chunks
¾ cup red wine
4 tbsp. tomato puree or paste
2 bay leaves
¼ tsp. cumin powder (or more if you like cumin)
¼ tsp. dried oregano leaves, crushed
¼ tsp. paprika
1½ tsp. salt
Dash black pepper
Pimento-stuffed olives (about 10)

Heat the oil in a pressure cooker.* Add the onion, garlic, and green and red peppers. Sauté for about a minute, turning constantly. Add the meat and sauté while adding the wine, tomato puree, and the rest of the ingredients.

*Add 2 ounces of water, and cover the cooker. When the valve indicates there is pressure, turn the heat down to medium, and cook for 30 minutes. Serve over white rice.

*Conventional Cooking Method

Heat the oil in a large Dutch oven or stockpot, and follow the rest of the recipe up to the second asterisk. Add 1½ cups of water, and ⅓ cup more wine. Reduce the heat to medium, and cook, covered, for approximately 1½ hours or until the meat is tender. Turn occasionally, and check the liquid, adding more if necessary.

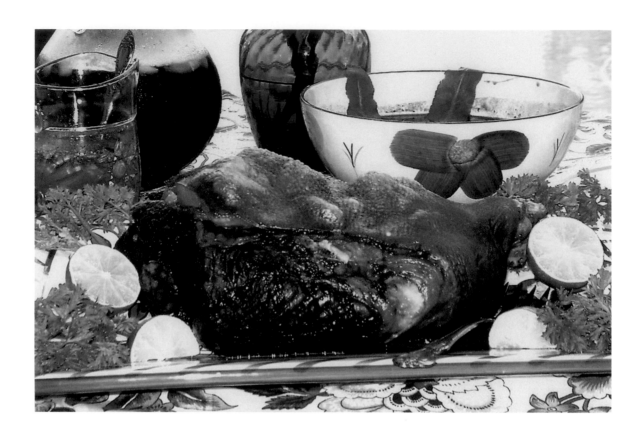

Roasted Pork Shoulder with Mojo Marinade

Paletica de Puerco Asada

This is an easy way to enjoy roast pork. This recipe will allow the cook to make a delicious, tender pork dish with very little effort. Follow the cooking instructions carefully. The secret to a "melt in your mouth" tender meat is to slow cook it in a low degree oven.

Serves 6 to 8

Pork
1 pork shoulder (7 to 9 lbs.)

Mojo
½ cup juice from sour oranges (if unavailable, add more vinegar and lime juice)
½ cup white vinegar
½ cup lime juice
8 or more garlic cloves, crushed
1 tsp. cumin powder
1 tsp. dried oregano leaves, crushed
1 tbsp. salt
½ tsp. black pepper

To prepare the **Pork,** wash the pork shoulder with water. Dry completely with paper towel (especially the skin). Place skin up on a roasting pan, and cook in a 250 degree oven. Use this formula to determine how long to cook the pork: 1 hour per lb. plus an extra ½ hour. For example, One 8 lb. shoulder = 8½ hours in 250 degree oven. Do *not* overcook.

When the time is up, turn the oven to broil, and broil for about 2 or 3 minutes, checking constantly. When the skin bubbles up, take it out immediately before it starts to burn. If the skin does burn, just scrape off the burnt part with a sharp knife. Wait 10 minutes before cutting to serve; this will help the skin become crispy.

Meanwhile, prepare the **Mojo.** Blend all ingredients together, and pour on the meat before serving. Leftover Mojo can be preserved in the refrigerator for several days. It is great on grilled steaks or chicken.

Note: Be patient and do *not* raise the temperature above 250 degrees. There is no need to check during the cooking process.

Note: More traditional Cuban recipes will have the Mojo inserted in the meat, by cutting small holes with a thin, sharp knife, and marinating the pork for about 10 hours before cooking it. After many years doing it that way, I found that the meat always needed more Mojo after cutting it, because the greater part of it did not have flavor. Now, I skip that step, and the results are great with less work.

Pork Leftovers in Spicy Tomato Sauce

Monteria

Monteria means "from the backcountry." This is a traditional Cuban dinner served on Christmas Day, made with the leftover meat from the roasted pig cooked on Christmas Eve.

Serves 4 to 6

3 tbsp. cooking oil
1 medium onion, chopped
5 large garlic cloves, mashed
½ green bell pepper, chopped
2 lbs. pork meat (leftover from the roast pork), cubed or shredded
½ cup red wine
¼ cup cooking wine
1 small can tomato paste (6 oz.)
1 can sweet red pimento with the liquid (7 oz.)
2 bay leaves
¼ tsp. cumin powder
¼ tsp. dried oregano leaves, crushed
Salt and black pepper to taste
10 pimento-stuffed olives
¾ cup raisins

In a large, deep skillet, heat the oil and add the onion, garlic, and the green peppers. Sauté until the onions are transparent. Add the pork meat and sauté while adding the wine, tomato paste, and the rest of the ingredients. Reduce the heat to medium-low, and simmer for approximately 20 minutes. Add more wine during cooking if the sauce gets dry; the sauce should be plenty juicy and abundant. Serve with white rice.

Pork Shoulder Pot Roast

Paleta de Cerdo Asada con Malta

1 small pork shoulder, around 7 to 8 lbs.
5 cloves
3 tbsp. cooking oil
1 onion, cut into slices
5 to 6 garlic cloves, mashed
½ tsp. cumin powder
¼ tsp. dry oregano
3 bay leaves
1 tbsp. salt
½ cup cooking wine
2 8-oz. bottles "Malta" soda (Dark, sweet malt beverage)

Wash the pork shoulder, and remove the skin. Save the skin to make fried pork rind *chicharrones*. Remove as much visible fat as possible. Stick the 5 cloves into the pork meat in different places of the shoulder. Heat the oil in a 6 qt. pressure cooker or large stockpot. Add the pork shoulder and brown on all sides. Add the onions, garlic, and the rest of the dry ingredients. Turn the pork shoulder a few more times to get the spices all over the meat, and add the wine. Open the 2 bottles of malta, wait for the foam to subside, and add them to the pork. Add 1 cup of water. When there is no more foam from the maltas, close the pressure cooker and wait for the pressure to build. Reduce the heat to medium, and cook for 1 hour and 15 minutes. If not using a pressure cooker, add 3 cups of water, close the pot, reduce the heat to medium, and cook for 2½ hours, or until tender. Slice the meat and serve on a deep platter, pouring the remaining sauce over it.

The skin can be cut into squares and deep fried until crispy to make *chicharrones*.

Fried Pork Meat

Masas de Puerco Fritas

Serves 4

2 lbs. lean pork meat, cut into chunks
6 large garlic cloves, mashed
Dash cumin powder
Salt to taste
Cooking oil
½ cup lime juice
¼ cup onion, thinly sliced

Rub the pork meat with 3 garlic cloves or ½ tsp. garlic salt. Season with the cumin powder and the salt. Do this step a few hours before cooking the meat and keep it refrigerated.

In a medium sauce pot, cook the meat in about 3 cups of water with the garlic and ½ teaspoon more of salt. Bring water to a boil, reduce the heat, cover, and simmer for about 1 hour. Drain the remaining water, remove the meat, and add enough cooking oil to be 1-inch deep. Heat the oil and return the pork meat to the hot oil. Fry over medium-high heat, turning it frequently, until the meat is golden brown. Remove from oil with a slotted spoon to drain and transfer to a serving plate. Mix the rest of the mashed garlic cloves with the lime juice, and pour on the meat. Garnish with the onion slices, and serve.

Pork Tenderloin Stuffed with Ham

Filete de Puerco Relleno con Jamon

Serves 6

Ham Stuffing
¼ cup onions, chopped
¼ cup red bell pepper, chopped
¾ lb. ground ham
1 hardboiled egg, chopped
8 or 9 pimento-stuffed olives, chopped
Dash black pepper
1 to 2 tbsp. cracker meal

Pork Tenderloin
1 pork tenderloin (can be cut in two)
3 tbsp. cooking oil
½ cup sliced Vidalia onions
5 to 6 mashed garlic cloves
½ tsp. cumin powder
½ tsp dry oregano
Salt and black pepper to taste
2 bay leaves
½ cup dry white wine or cooking wine
¼ cup sherry wine or Marsala wine

To prepare the **Ham Stuffing,** place the onions and bell peppers in a food processor, and process on a slow speed until mashed. Mix the rest of the ingredients in a bowl, adding the onion/bell pepper mash, until a smooth paste is formed. Spoon the stuffing into a pastry bag with a simple, long tip.

To prepare the **Pork Tenderloin,** wash the tenderloin and dry it with paper towels. Rub the meat with some of the mashed garlic, cumin powder, oregano, salt, and pepper. With a thin, sharp, paring knife, cut a slit lengthwise through the center of the pork, but do not cut all the way through the pork—this is where the stuffing will go. Add another slit, forming an X through the center of the pork. Insert the tip of the pastry bag with the stuffing into the hole made with the knife, and fill it with as much stuffing as possible.

Heat the oil in a 6 qt. pressure cooker.* Add the onion slices and the rest of the garlic. Add the pork tenderloin and brown on all sides, while adding the rest of the dry ingredients. Add the wines, turning the meat a few more times.

Finally, add 2 cups of water. Close the pressure cooker, wait for the pressure to build, and reduce the heat to medium. Cook for 30 minutes. When the pressure is gone, open the cooker and transfer the tenderloin to a serving platter. Cut into ½-inch slices. Return the cooking juices to the heat, and simmer until reduced. Pour on the meat before serving.

*Conventional Cooking Method
Heat the oil in a large Dutch oven or stockpot, adding all the ingredients as instructed above. Then, add 3 cups of water, reduce the heat to medium, and cook for 1 hour. Transfer to a serving platter. Cut into ½-inch slices. Return the cooking juices to the heat, and simmer until reduced. Pour on the meat before serving.

Ham Hocks with Cabbage and Potatoes

Lacon con Papas y Col

This is another recipe imported from Spain. It is not as well known as the Flan or Paella.

Serves 4 to 6

2 lbs. ham hocks
½ yellow or Vidalia onion
2 medium potatoes, peeled and
    cut into chunks
½ cabbage, cut into chunks
1 medium white onion, sliced
Olive oil (about ¼ cup)
3 to 4 tbsp. vinegar

In a 6 qt. or larger pressure cooker,* place the ham hocks with the yellow onion, cover with water, and turn the heat to high. Cover the cooker and wait for the pressure to build. Reduce the heat to medium and cook for 1 hour. When the pressure is off, open the pressure cooker.

In that same water, boil the potatoes and the cabbage until cooked; potatoes should be tender but firm. There is no need to add salt, because this water is salty and very flavorful. Use a regular lid to cover lightly while cooking. Drain the ham hocks, and cut into smaller pieces, as much as possible. Drain the potatoes and the cabbage, and transfer to a large serving platter. Add the pieces of ham hocks and the slices of white onions. Pour the olive oil on top and add the vinegar.

*Conventional Cooking Method

In a large Dutch oven or stockpot, cook the ham hocks with the onions in about 6 cups of water. Bring to a boil, reduce the heat to medium, and cook for 2½ hours. Continue with the above instructions from adding potatoes and cabbage.

Pigs' Feet in Spicy Tomato Sauce

Paticas de Puerco Estilo Fricase

Serves 4

2 lbs. pigs' feet, cut into 2 to 4 pieces each
3 tbsp. cooking oil
1 medium onion, chopped
6 large garlic cloves, mashed
1 Spanish sausage (chorizo) cut into ½-in. slices
½ red bell pepper, chopped
½ green bell pepper, chopped
¾ cup red wine or dry cooking wine
1 small can tomato puree or paste
2 bay leaves
¼ tsp. cumin powder (can use more if desired)
¼ tsp. dried oregano leaves, crushed
¼ tsp. paprika
1½ tsp. salt
¼ tsp. black pepper
¼ tsp. crushed red pepper
Pimento-stuffed olives (about 10)
½ cup raisins (1 box)

In the pressure cooker,* cook the pigs' feet in 4 cups of water and some salt for 30 minutes. Begin counting the minutes after the pressure builds. Discard the water afterwards, but leave the pigs' feet in the cooker. Heat the oil in a separate pan. Add the onion, garlic, chorizo, and red and green bell peppers. Sauté for about a minute, turning constantly. Add the wine, tomato puree, and the rest of the ingredients. Sauté for about 2 more minutes, and turn off the heat. Pour this sauce over the pigs' feet, and turn several times to coat the meat completely. *Add ½ cup of water, and cover the cooker. When the valve indicates there is pressure, turn the heat down to medium, and cook for 30 minutes. Serve with white rice and ripe, fried plantains.

Conventional Cooking Method

Use a large Dutch oven or stockpot, instead of the pressure cooker. Bring the water with the pigs' feet to a boil, reduce heat to medium-high, and cook for 1 hour. Discard the water, and continue with the rest of the recipe to the second asterisk. After adding the sautéed ingredients to the pigs' feet, add one cup of water, and cook over medium-high heat for about 1 hour. Turn occasionally, checking the liquid and adding more wine or water if necessary. The sauce should be juicy and abundant. Serve with white rice and ripe, fried plantains.

Elbow Macaroni with Ham and Spanish Sausage

Macarrones con Jamon y Chorizo

Serves 2 to 4

3 tbsp. olive oil
½ onion, finely chopped
¼ green or red bell pepper, chopped
4 or 5 garlic cloves, mashed
1 lb. smoked ham, cut into small cubes
1 Spanish sausage (chorizo), cut into thin slices
3 tbsp. tomato paste or puree
¼ cup cooking wine
½ tsp. salt
Dash cumin powder
Dash dry oregano
Dash black pepper
1 box elbow macaroni (16 oz.)
½ cup milk

In a deep saucepot, heat the oil. Add the onions, bell peppers, garlic, ham, and Spanish sausage. Sauté until the onions are transparent. Add the tomato paste or puree, wine, and spices, stirring constantly. Add 1½ cups of water, mix everything, and bring to a boil. Add the macaroni, reduce the heat to medium, and cook for 7 minutes. Add the milk, and cook for another 5 minutes, or until the pasta is tender and the sauce thickens. Stir often while cooking, to prevent it from sticking to the bottom.

Sirloin Steak Cuban Style

Bistek de Palomilla

Serves 4

4 sirloin steaks, thinly sliced
4 garlic cloves, mashed
Salt and black pepper to taste
3 tbsp. cooking oil
½ cup white onion, chopped;
    plus a few more slices of onion
Vinegar
¼ cup chopped fresh parsley
Lime wedges

Wash the steaks and dry them with a paper towel. Place in a shallow dish. Rub the steaks with 2 mashed garlic cloves, and sprinkle them with a dash of salt and pepper. Allow to marinate for a couple of hours, or longer, in the refrigerator. Right before dinner, heat oil in a frying pan. Add the slices of onion, and the 2 other mashed garlic cloves. Immediately add the steaks, and fry on high for about one minute on each side, or until you reach desired doneness. The meat will be juicier if pink inside. Sprinkle a little vinegar on the steaks, and serve immediately. Garnish with the chopped onions and parsley. Serve with lime wedges, and squeeze a little lime juice on the steaks before eating.

Variation: Mojo Marinade
    You can also make a simple Mojo for the steaks by mixing the lime juice with some mashed garlic cloves, and pouring it on the steaks before serving them.

Breaded Steak

Bistek Empanizado

Serves 4

4 sirloin steaks thinly sliced (top round steaks may also be used)
4 garlic cloves, mashed or dash garlic powder
Salt to taste
1 cup cracker meal (approximately)
2 eggs, beaten
¼ cup cooking oil
½ cup onion slices
Lime wedges

Wash the steaks and dry them with a paper towel. Place in a shallow dish. Rub each steak with a mashed garlic clove and sprinkle with a dash of salt, or sprinkle with garlic powder. Spread the cracker meal on a large platter or a large piece of plastic wrap. Put the beaten eggs in a shallow bowl. Press each steak into the cracker meal first, then the eggs, and then the cracker meal again, pressing down firmly, to ensure the breading sticks to every part of the steak. Heat the oil in a large frying pan. Add a few slices of onion. Immediately add the steaks, two at a time, and fry on medium-high heat until golden brown and crispy. Place them on paper towels to drain off the excess oil. Garnish with the rest of the onion slices. Serve with lime wedges, and squeeze lime juice on the steaks before eating.

Note: If the oil gets too full of burnt crumbs, clean with a strainer, and add more oil to fry the other 2 steaks.

Refried Shredded Beef
Vaca Frita

Serves 4

1½ lbs. skirt or flank steak, cut crosswise
   in 2-inch strips
1 onion, cut in half
½ green pepper, cut into 2 pieces
1 tbsp. salt
4 tbsp. cooking oil
1 medium onion, cut into thin slices
5 to 6 large garlic cloves, mashed
¼ tsp. cumin powder
Dash dry oregano
Lime or lemon juice

In a pressure cooker,* boil the meat in 6 cups of water, with the onion cut in half, the green bell pepper, and salt for 1 hour. Start timing after the pressure has built. After the pressure is down, open the cooker, take out the meat, and let it cool.

Shred the meat with a fork and knife or with your hands. Heat oil in large skillet; add onion and garlic, and sauté for about 1 minute. Add the shredded beef and sauté, scraping the pan to prevent it from sticking; add more oil if necessary. Add the cumin and the oregano, sprinkling them on the meat while turning it. Cook until the meat is brown, but do *not* burn. Meat should feel slightly crunchy when eating it. Remove from heat and serve. Sprinkle with lime or lemon juice, and add more salt if necessary. This meat dish is usually served with white rice and black beans.

*Conventional Cooking Method
  Use a large Dutch oven or stockpot to boil the meat with the onion, green pepper, and salt in 6 to 8 cups of water. Cover and cook for 2½ to 3 hours, or until the meat is very tender. Continue with above recipe, beginning with shredding the meat.

Shredded Beef

Ropa Vieja

This is one of the most popular and well known Cuban dishes. It is widely known by its Spanish name *Ropa Vieja,* which means "old clothes," because it resembles the torn threads of worn fabric.

Serves 4

Beef

1½ lbs. beef (skirt or flank steak), cut crosswise into approximately 2-inch strips
1 onion, cut in half
½ green pepper, cut into 2 parts
1 tbsp. salt

Sauce

3 tbsp. cooking oil
1 medium onion, cut into thin slices
5 large garlic cloves, mashed
½ green pepper, cut in thin slices
½ cup red wine or dry cooking wine
¼ tsp. ground cumin
¼ tsp. dry oregano
Dash black pepper
½ can tomato paste (6 oz. can)
Beef broth
10 pimento-stuffed olives

To prepare the **Beef,** boil the meat with the onion, green pepper, and salt, for 1 hour and 15 minutes in a pressure cooker.* Start timing after the pressure is built. When the pressure is gone, take the meat out and let it cool.

Shred the meat with a fork and knife or your hands. Reserve the broth.

To make **Sauce,** heat oil in a deep skillet; add onions, garlic, and green peppers. Sauté until the onions are transparent. Add the shredded beef and the rest of the ingredients, while turning constantly. Add about 1 cup of the broth, lower the heat, cover, and simmer for about 15 minutes. Check the taste, and add more salt if necessary. If it dries too much, add more broth. Serve with rice.

*Conventional Cooking Method

Use a large Dutch oven or stockpot to boil the meat with the onion, green pepper, and salt in 6 to 8 cups of water. Cover and cook for 2½ to 3 hours, or until the meat is very tender. Cool, shred, and continue with the sauce recipe as directed above.

Pot Roast

Boliche

Serves 6

1 *Boliche* (top round roast, about 3 lbs.)
2 tsp. salt
¼ tsp cumin powder
¼ tsp dry oregano leaves, crushed
1 Spanish sausage (chorizo)
¼ cup cooking oil
1 onion, chopped (save some slices for the skillet)
6 to 8 large garlic cloves, mashed (save a few for the skillet)
3 bay leaves
Dash black pepper
¾ cup cooking or red, table wine (plus ¼ cup for the skillet)
1 can tomato paste (save half for the skillet; 6 oz. can)
1 can sweet red pimentos, sliced, for the skillet (7 oz. can)
4 tbsp. vinegar (for the skillet)
Pimento-stuffed olives (for the skillet)

Season the meat with 1 tsp. of salt, the cumin, and the oregano a few hours before cooking. Cut 2 crossing slits in the center of the meat, from one end to the other, and stuff with a Spanish sausage (chorizo) before cooking.

In a pressure cooker,* heat 4 tbsp. of oil. Place the meat in the hot oil and brown on all sides while adding the onions, garlic, bay leaves, the rest of the salt, black pepper, wine, and ½ of the tomato paste. Make sure all sides of the meat are embedded in the seasonings. *Add enough water to cover more than half of the meat, close the pressure cooker and wait until the vent valve goes up. Lower the heat to medium and cook for 1 hour.

After the meat is done, allow it to cool completely, and place in refrigerator for 1 hour; this can be left overnight, also. Cut into ½ to ¾-inch slices. Heat 3 tbsp. of oil in a large skillet. Place the slices of meat in skillet with the reserved slices of onions, mashed garlic, the can of red pimentos, the rest of the tomato paste, and ¼ cup of wine. Sprinkle with a little more cumin and oregano. Check the taste, and add more salt if needed. Sauté for 1 or 2 minutes, turning once, making sure both sides of the meat are covered by the sauce. Sprinkle with the vinegar, add the olives, and serve.

Conventional Cooking Method
Heat the oil in a large Dutch oven or stockpot, and follow the recipe up to the second asterisk. Add enough water to cover more than half of the meat. Bring to a boil, cover, and reduce the heat to medium. Cook for 3 hours or until the meat is tender. Continue with the above recipe, beginning with cooling the meat.

Beef Stew

Carne Con Papas

Serves 4

3 tbsp. cooking oil
1 medium onion, chopped
5 to 6 large garlic cloves, mashed
¼ green bell pepper, chopped
¼ red bell pepper, chopped
2 lbs. lean beef, cut into chunks
  (chuck or skirt beef)
¾ cup red wine
4 tbsp. tomato paste or puree
1 large potato, peeled and cut
  into chunks
2 carrots, cut into slices
2 bay leaves
¼ tsp. cumin powder
¼ tsp. dried oregano leaves,
  crushed
¼ tsp. paprika
1½ tsp. salt
Dash black pepper
Pimento-stuffed olives (about 10)
Handful of raisins (optional)

Heat the oil in a pressure cooker.* Add the onions, garlic, and red and green bell peppers. Sauté for about a minute, turning constantly. Add the meat and sauté while adding the wine, tomato puree or paste, and the rest of the ingredients. *Add ½ cup of water, and cover the cooker. When the valve indicates there is pressure, turn the heat down to medium, and cook for 35 minutes. Wait until the pressure is gone, open, and serve.

Conventional Cooking Method

Heat the oil in a large Dutch oven or stockpot, and follow the recipe up to the second asterisk. Add 1½ cups of water, and ¼ cup more wine. Reduce the heat to medium, and cook, covered, for approximately 1½ hours or until the meat is tender. Turn occasionally, and check the liquid; add more water if necessary.

Meatloaf

Salpicon

Serves 4 to 6

2 celery stalks cut in small sections (optional)
1 onion, cut into chunks
4 garlic cloves, peeled or garlic powder
¼ green or red bell pepper
1 egg
3 slices bread, soaked in milk
1 lb. lean ground beef
1 lb. lean ground pork
¼ tsp. cumin powder
Dash oregano
Dash black pepper
1 tsp. salt
2 tbsp. Worcestershire sauce
Cracker meal or bread crumbs
BBQ sauce (I prefer Honey Hickory)

In a blender, put the celery, onions, garlic, bell pepper, egg, and the bread soaked in milk. Blend at a low speed until smooth. Place the ground meats in a large bowl, and pour the mixture on it. Add the seasonings and Worcestershire sauce. Knead with your hands thoroughly while sprinkling in the cracker meal to give it consistency. Place in a 9" x 4" glass baking pan or any bread-baking pan. Bake for 50 minutes in a 350 degree oven. Remove pan from the oven, and pour the BBQ sauce on top of the meatloaf. Bake for another 10 to 15 minutes.

Time Saving Tip: Use an envelope of onion soup in place of the onions, garlic, green bell pepper, cumin, and salt. Bake in a microwave oven for 13 minutes, then pour the BBQ sauce on it. Bake in a regular or toaster oven for 20 minutes.

Picadillo

Ground Beef

This versatile ground beef recipe is the main part of many other recipes throughout this cookbook, including "Meat Pastries" and "Shepherd's Pie."

Serves 4

2 tbsp. cooking oil
1 medium onion, finely chopped
5 large garlic cloves, mashed
¼ green bell pepper, chopped
¼ red bell pepper, chopped
1½ lbs. lean ground beef (Can use ground turkey instead)
½ cup red wine or cooking wine
½ can tomato paste (6 oz. can)
¼ tsp. cumin powder
¼ tsp. dried oregano leaves, crushed
1 tsp. salt
Dash black pepper
Red-pimento stuffed olives
½ cup raisins (optional)

Heat oil in deep skillet or 2 qt. saucepot. Add the onions, garlic, and bell peppers; sauté for about 1 minute. Add the ground beef and sauté, breaking apart the lumps as much as possible. Add the wine, tomato paste, and the rest of the ingredients while continuing to stir. Lower the heat, and simmer for approximately 20 minutes. If it dries up, add more wine. Dish should be saucy.

Variation: Shepherd's Pie

Cook the ground beef as indicated above, but cut the tomato paste to only 1 tbsp., and cut the wine to ¼ cup. Do not use olives. Add some vegetables of your choice, such as carrots, corn, and celery. Cook over medium/high heat until the liquid has evaporated, turning constantly. Transfer to a glass baking dish. Cover with mashed potatoes and a layer of Parmesan cheese. Bake in a 325 degree oven until the cheese melts and turns golden brown.

Lasagna Speciale
Lasaña Especial

The Cuban influence in this very rich Italian recipe is evident by the use of 2 "special" ingredients: ground pork, and my favorite spice—cumin!

Yields about 15 servings

Lasagna
3 tbsp. olive oil
½ lb. Italian sausage
1 lb. ground pork
1 lb. lean ground beef
1 large onion, finely chopped
6 to 8 garlic cloves, peeled and crushed
½ green and ½ red bell peppers, chopped
⅓ cup Marsala wine (dry)
1 small can tomato paste (6 oz.)
1 can tomato puree (11 oz.)
1 can diced tomatoes (15 oz.)
¾ cup red table wine
⅓ tsp. dried oregano leaves, crushed
¼ tsp. cumin powder
¼ to ½ tsp. crushed red pepper
2 bay leaves
2½ tsp. salt
Dash thyme
Dash black pepper
1 box pasta for lasagna (16 oz.)
2½ lbs. Mozzarella cheese, shredded
1 lb. mixed Romano and Parmesan cheeses, grated
1 large container Ricotta cheese, whole or low fat (32 oz.)
1 egg, beaten
2 cups grated Reggiano Parmesan cheese

To prepare the **Lasagna,** in a large Dutch oven or 12-inch-deep skillet, heat the olive oil. Cut a slit on the side of the Italian sausages, and peel off the skin. Crumble the meat as much as possible, placing it in the oil. Sauté, separating the meat as you would ground beef. Add the ground pork and ground beef, continuing to cook for about 3 minutes until the meat is half cooked and crumbled. Add the minced onion, crushed garlic cloves, and chopped green and red bell peppers, and continue to sauté. Add the Marsala wine and sauté. Add the cans of tomato paste, tomato puree, and diced tomatoes. Keep stirring while it cooks. Add the red wine and the spices to make the meat sauce for the lasagna. Add ½ cup of water. Reduce the heat to low, and leave covered, turning occasionally.

Boil the pasta in a large pot in salted water; it should taste like sea water. Cook according to package directions. Pour a little bit of oil in the water to prevent the foam from spilling over; turn occasionally to prevent sticking.

White Sauce
3 tbsp. unsalted butter
Dash white pepper
1 envelope onion soup
2 heaping tbsp. flour
1½ cups milk

In the meantime, to prepare the **White Sauce,** melt the butter in a 2 qt. sauce pan. Add the white pepper, onion soup, and flour, turning quickly to form a ball that separates from the sides of the pan. Add the milk at once, and continue to turn until the sauce thickens to the consistency of a pudding. Remove from heat.

In a rectangular 13" by 9" or 3 qt. glass pan, start assembling the lasagna by pouring about ½ cup of the meat sauce in the bottom of the pan. Follow with a layer of the pasta, a layer of half the meat sauce, a layer of Mozzarella cheese, and a thin layer of the Romano/Parmesan cheese. Follow with another layer of the pasta. Next, mix the Ricotta cheese with the beaten egg and spread carefully on the pasta; pour the white sauce over the Ricotta. Follow with a layer of Mozzarella cheese, and a thin layer of Romano/Parmesan cheeses. Follow with the last layer of pasta; add the remaining meat sauce; top with Mozzarella cheese, and sprinkle the Reggiano Parmesan cheese last. Bake the lasagna in 350 degree oven for 30 minutes. Allow to cool for 25 minutes before cutting to serve.

Note: On some occasions, I have mixed the ricotta cheese with the white sauce before spreading it on the pasta. This makes for a very creamy lasagna, but sometimes the cream overflows when the lasagna is being cut to be served.

Stuffed Bell Peppers

Ajies Rellenos

Serves 4

Stuffing
1 medium onion, cut into chunks
3 large garlic cloves, peeled
¼ red bell pepper, cut into chunks
2 tbsp. cooking oil
1 lb. lean ground beef
½ lb. ground pork
¼ cup red wine or cooking wine
3 tbsp. tomato paste
7 or 8 pimento-stuffed olives, chopped
¼ tsp. cumin powder
¼ tsp. dried oregano leaves, crushed
1 tsp. salt
Dash black pepper
4 green bell peppers (perfectly shaped with even bottoms)

Sauce
3 tbsp. olive oil
1 medium onion, chopped
5 garlic cloves mashed
½ can tomato paste or puree (6 oz. can)
½ cup red wine or cooking wine
¼ tsp. cumin powder
¼ tsp. dried oregano leaves, crushed
1 tsp. salt
Dash black pepper and red crushed pepper

To prepare the **Stuffing,** place the onions, garlic, and red bell peppers in a food processor, and process until pureed. Heat oil in a deep skillet or 2 qt. saucepot. Add the ground beef and ground pork and sauté while breaking apart the lumps completely. Add the mixture from the food processor, and add the wine, tomato paste, and the rest of the ingredients while stirring. Reduce the heat to low, and simmer for approximately 20 minutes.

Cut off the top of the green bell peppers one inch from the stem and remove carefully. Wash the inside with water, removing all the seeds and white sections. Fill each pepper with the ground beef mixture. Place the top back on and set aside.

To prepare the **Sauce,** heat the olive oil in a deep saucepot. Add the onions and the garlic. Sauté until the onions are transparent. Add the rest of the ingredients, plus 1 cup of water. Stir the sauce, and start placing the stuffed bell peppers in the pot carefully, by letting them stand with some space between them, but not too much. Cover the pot, and cook on low heat until the bell peppers appear tender, about 20 to 25 minutes.

Variation: Stuffed Bell Peppers with Rice
Add 1 cup of cooked white rice to the beef mix before stuffing the bell peppers.

Kibbe

Kibbe is a dish from the Lebanese community present in Cuba during the years before the 1960s. As a child, I used to watch my uncle make Kibbe with a giant mortar and pestle, where the meat was "cooked" using lime juice and beating on it for hours. It was then eaten raw or fried in patties. This last one is the recipe I am including here.

Serves 6 to 8

Meat Patties
4 cups bulgur (cracked wheat)
2 large onions
2 red bell peppers
4 to 6 mint leaves
3 lbs. lean ground beef
½ tsp. allspice (sweet pepper)
Salt and black pepper to taste
Olive oil (enough to fry)

Meat Filling
Olive oil
½ lb. pork meat, cut into tiny cubes
½ lb. beef, cut into tiny cubes
1 large onion, finely chopped
1 red bell pepper, finely chopped
1 tsp. salt
Dash black pepper
2 tbsp. olives, chopped (more if desired)
2 tbsp. raisins (more if desired)
¼ tsp. cumin powder
¼ tsp. dry oregano
Juice from 1 lime

To make the **Meat Patties,** soak the bulgur in water for 1 hour. In a food processor, place the onions, bell peppers, and mint, and process until smooth. Add the 3 lbs. of ground beef, the bulgur, and the rest of the spices; grind together. Transfer to a large bowl. Wet your hands with water and form 5-inch-wide patties from this mixture.

To make the **Meat Filling,** sauté all the ingredients for the meat filling—except lime juice—in olive oil, until the meats are browned and completely cooked. Remove from heat, and add the lime juice.

Fill each patty with a tablespoon of the "meat filling" and top with another patty. Press the edges to seal together. Fry the patties in olive oil over medium heat, turning them once, and trying to scrape the bottom to prevent them from sticking too much. Cook until the meat is brown on both sides.

Meatballs in Tomato Sauce

Albondigas en Salsa de Tomate

Serves 4

Meatballs
1 small onion or ½ Vidalia onion,
     cut into chunks
4 garlic cloves, peeled or garlic
     powder
¼ green and red bell peppers
1 egg
2 slices bread, soaked in milk
1 lb. lean ground beef
½ lb. lean ground pork
Dash black pepper
1 tsp. salt
2 tbsp. Worcestershire sauce
Cracker meal or bread crumbs

Tomato Sauce
3 tbsp. olive oil
½ Vidalia or Spanish onion,
     chopped
½ cup red and green bell pep-
     pers, chopped
4 to 5 garlic cloves, mashed
1 small can tomato paste (6 oz.)
¼ tsp. cumin powder
¼ tsp. dry oregano
Dash crushed red pepper
½ cup red wine or cooking wine
1 cup water

To prepare the **Meatballs,** put the onions, garlic, bell pepper, egg, and the bread soaked in milk in a blender. Blend at a low speed until smooth. Place the ground meats in a large bowl, and pour the mixture in. Add the seasonings and Worcestershire sauce. Knead with your hands thoroughly while sprinkling with cracker meal to give it consistency. Wet your hands with water, and shape the meatballs. They should be 1 to 1½ inches in diameter.

To make the **Tomato Sauce,** heat the oil in a large, deep skillet and sauté the onions, bell peppers, and garlic over high heat until the onions are translucent. Add the rest of the ingredients, and stir until well blended.

Place the meatballs in the sauce, lower the heat to medium/low, and cook for about 25 minutes, stirring occasionally and scraping the bottom. Lower the heat if the meatballs are sticking to the bottom of the pan. Larger meatballs require longer cooking time. Serve over white rice or pasta.

Oxtail on Fire (In Spicy Tomato Sauce)

Rabo Encendido

This recipe calls for a great deal of hot spice. The amount of red pepper can be increased, or decreased to suit personal tastes. However, it is recommended that extra hot sauce be made available at the table, for those who want a spicy taste!

Serves 4

3 lbs. oxtail, cut up in sections
1 tsp. salt
2 tbsp. cooking oil
1 large onion, chopped
6 to 8 large garlic cloves, mashed
½ green bell pepper, chopped
½ red bell pepper, chopped
1½ cups red wine
¼ cup dry sherry
1 can tomato puree or paste (6 oz.)
1 cup water
2 tsp. salt
3 bay leaves
⅓ tsp. cumin powder
⅓ tsp. dried oregano leaves, crushed
¼ tsp. paprika
¼ tsp. black pepper
½ tsp. crushed red pepper
Dash thyme
Pimento-stuffed olives (about 10)

In the pressure cooker,* cook the oxtail in enough water to cover the meat and 1 tsp. salt for 40 minutes; count the minutes after the pressure builds. Discard the water afterwards. This process removes a great deal of fat. *Heat the oil in a large, deep skillet. Add the onions, garlic, and the red and green bell peppers. Sauté for about 1 minute, turning constantly. Add the meat, wine, tomato puree or paste, and the rest of the ingredients. Keep stirring to cover the meat with the sauce. Reduce the heat to low, and simmer for approximately 1 hour. Check the salt, and add more if necessary. Add a little water if the sauce seems too dry; the sauce should be plenty. Serve with white rice.

Conventional Cooking Method

Use a large Dutch oven or stockpot. Add the meat with enough water to cover, and bring to a boil. Reduce the heat to medium, and cook, covered, for 1 hour. Discard the water, and continue with the rest of the recipe from the second asterisk.

Shredded, Salted Dry Beef

Tasajo

Tasajo can be purchased in Cuban food markets. Traditionally, *tasajo* was made from buffalo or horse meat. It was salted and dried by smoking the meat or leaving it out in the sun for several days. This process allowed the meat to be stored without refrigeration, which was non-existent then, for a long period of time. Dry, salted beef (skirt or flank) can be substituted instead.

Serves 4 to 6

Shredded Beef
1½ lbs. salted dry beef (*tasajo*)
1 onion, cut in half
½ green pepper, cut in 2 pieces

Sauce
3 tbsp. cooking oil
1 medium onion, cut in thin slices
6 to 7 large garlic cloves, mashed
½ green or red (or both) bell pepper, cut in thin slices
¾ cup red wine (Do not use cooking wine because it has salt)
¼ tsp. ground cumin
¼ tsp. dry oregano
Dash black pepper
½ can tomato paste (6 oz.)
Pimento-stuffed olives

To prepare the **Shredded Beef,** soak the meat in water for about 30 minutes. Drain the beef and discard the water. Place in fresh water again, soak for another 30 minutes, and drain. Repeat this process several times, to remove the excess salt.

In a pressure cooker,* boil the meat with the onion and the green pepper for 1 hour. Start timing after the pressure has been reached. When the pressure is gone, take the meat out and let it cool. Rinse with cool running water to help take out the salt imbedded in the meat. Cut off excess fat, and shred the meat with your hands or two forks.

To prepare the **Sauce,** heat the oil in a deep skillet; add onions, garlic, and bell peppers. Sauté until the onions become transparent. Add the shredded meat and the rest of the ingredients, while turning constantly. Lower the heat and simmer, covered, for about 25 minutes. If during this time the sauce dries up, add half a cup of water, or a little more wine. Serve with white rice.

*Conventional Cooking Method
In a large Dutch oven or stockpot, boil the meat with 6 to 8 cups of water for 2 hours, or until tender. Drain the meat. Rinse with cool, running water to help take out the salt imbedded in the meat. Cut off excess fat, and shred the meat with your hands or two forks. Continue with the **Sauce** preparation.

Okra Stew

Quimbombo

Although this can be served as a side dish, it can also be an entrée. Given the amount of meat used, I have decided to include it as an entrée.

Serves 4

2 lbs. okra (fresh or frozen)
Vinegar for soaking
3 to 4 tbsp. olive oil or cooking oil
1 onion, chopped
½ cup green and/or red bell peppers, chopped
5 to 6 garlic cloves, mashed
1 lb. pork, cut into small chunks (may be substituted with ground beef)
1 tsp. salt
2 bay leaves
½ small can tomato paste or puree (6 oz.)
¼ tsp. cumin powder
Dash black pepper
Dash red pepper (optional)
¼ cup cooking wine or table wine
½ cup water

Wash okra thoroughly; cut and discard the stem end. Cut the okra into 1-inch chunks. Soak the okra in water with some vinegar, to remove the slimy feel. After one or two hours, drain the okra, and cover with fresh water and vinegar again. Boil in that water for 3 to 5 minutes. Drain and rinse.

Heat the oil in a deep sauce pot. Add the onions, bell peppers, and garlic. Sauté until the onions are translucent. Add the pork, and the rest of the seasonings, while turning. Add the wine and the ½ cup water. Check the taste, and add more salt if necessary. Lower the heat to medium/low, and simmer for 20 minutes. Add the okra, and continue to cook until both the meat and the okra are tender, about 15 minutes. If the mixture gets too dry, add more water or wine. Serve over white rice.

Lamb Stew

Chilindron

Serves 4

2 lbs. lamb meat, cut into chunks with excess fat removed
1 cup red wine
3 tbsp. cooking oil
1 large onion, chopped
6 to 8 garlic cloves, mashed
½ green bell pepper, chopped
½ red bell pepper, chopped (optional)
¼ cup sherry or Marsala wine
½ cup red wine
½ can tomato puree or paste (6 oz.)
3 bay leaves
¼ tsp. cumin powder
¼ tsp. dried oregano leaves, crushed
Pinch thyme
¼ tsp. paprika
¼ tsp. black pepper
1½ tsp. salt
¼ tsp. crushed red pepper
Pimento-stuffed olives (about 10)

Marinate the lamb in the red wine for several hours before cooking, turning occasionally. When you are ready to cook, heat the oil in a pressure cooker.* Add the onions, garlic, and red and green peppers. Sauté for about a minute, turning constantly. Add the meat with the wine and sauté while adding the other wines, tomato puree or paste, and the rest of the ingredients. Check the taste, and add more salt if necessary. *Add ½ cup water, and cover the cooker. When the valve indicates there is pressure, turn the heat down to medium, and cook for 35 minutes. When you open the cooker, check if it is too watery. Simmer for a few minutes, uncovered, until the sauce thickens. If there is not enough liquid, add a little more wine. Serve with white rice.

Conventional Cooking Method

Heat the oil in a large Dutch oven or stockpot, and follow the above recipe up to the second asterisk. Add 1½ cups of water and ½ cup more wine to the pot. Reduce the heat to medium and cook, covered, for approximately 1½ hours, or until the meat is tender. Turn occasionally, and check the liquid; add more if necessary.

Moussaka

This is an outstanding recipe, originally from Greece. It uses ground lamb meat, but it can also be made with a mixture of ground pork and beef for a Cuban take on the dish.

Serves 6

Moussaka
2 medium eggplants
Olive oil
1 medium onion, finely chopped
2 lbs. lean, ground lamb meat
6 large garlic cloves, mashed
½ can tomato paste (6 oz.)
½ cup red wine
¼ cup Marsala wine
2 tsp. ground cinnamon
1½ tsp. salt
¼ tsp. black pepper
2 bay leaves
1 clove, crushed
½ tsp. dried oregano, crushed

Cheese Sauce
¼ cup butter
3 tbsp. all purpose flour
1 tsp. salt
¼ tsp. ground nutmeg
1¾ cups milk
3 beaten eggs
15 oz. ricotta cheese
1 cup grated Parmesan cheese
Bread crumbs

To prepare the **Moussaka,** cut eggplants into ¼-inch slices. Brush slices lightly with oil and place on broiler pan. Broil 6 inches from heat for 10 to 12 minutes or until tender, turning once. Drain on paper towel and season with salt. In a skillet, heat the oil and sauté the onions and meat until brown, turning and breaking up the meat. Stir in tomato paste, wines, cinnamon, salt, and the other spices. Simmer until the liquid evaporates somewhat.

To prepare **Cheese Sauce,** melt butter in a medium saucepan. Blend in the flour, salt, and the nutmeg. Turn quickly, making a ball that separates from the sides. Add milk all at once. Cook and stir until thickened and bubbly. Remove from heat. Gradually add the beaten eggs, ricotta cheese and parmesan cheese; blend well.

Sprinkle bread crumbs in the bottom of a 13" by 9" glass baking pan. Layer half the eggplant, all the meat mixture, and then the remaining eggplant. Pour cheese sauce on top. Bake, uncovered, in 350 degree oven for 40 to 50 minutes. Let stand 5 to 10 minutes before cutting to serve.

Beef Tongue Stew
Lengua Estofada

Serves 4 to 6

1 beef tongue
1 tbsp. salt
4 tbsp. olive oil or cooking oil
1 onion, chopped
½ cup green or red bell peppers
6 to 8 large garlic cloves, mashed
1 can tomato puree or paste (6 oz.)
½ can red pimentos (7 oz. can)
¾ cup red table wine
8 to 10 pimento-stuffed olives (optional)
2 dry bay leaves
¼ tsp. cumin powder
¼ tsp. dry oregano leaves, crushed
Dash black pepper
Dash red pepper
Splash vinegar

Place tongue in the pressure cooker.* Cover with water and add the salt. Close the pressure cooker, turn the heat to high, and wait until the vent valve goes up. Lower the heat to medium, and cook for 45 minutes. After the pressure is gone, take out the tongue, and discard the liquid.

Cut the outer skin off the tongue, exposing the lean meat inside. Discard the skin. Cut the meat into ½-inch slices. Heat the oil in a large, deep skillet. Add the onions, bell peppers, and garlic. Sauté until the onions are becoming translucent. Add the tomato paste or puree, red pimentos, wine, olives, and all the spices. Place the slices of meat in the skillet with the sauce, turning several times to make sure the meat is covered by the sauce. Check the salt level, and add more if necessary. Simmer on low heat, covered, for approximately 30 minutes. Splash with vinegar before serving.

*Conventional Cooking Method

Place beef tongue in a large Dutch oven or stockpot. Cover with water, and add the salt. Bring to a boil, reduce the heat to medium, and cook for 2 hours. Take out the tongue, and discard the liquid. Proceed with the recipe as directed above.

Sweetbread Fritters

Frituras de Seso

Yields 8 to 10 fritters

½ lb. beef or pork brain (sweetbreads)
1 egg
2 tbsp. chopped parsley
1 or 2 tbsp. flour
Dash white pepper
Dash black pepper
1 tsp. salt
Oil for deep frying

Rinse sweetbreads and transfer to a 4-qt. saucepan. Add enough cold water to cover sweetbreads by 1 inch. Bring to a boil, reduce heat, and simmer, uncovered, until sweetbreads plump and feel slightly firmer to the touch, about 10 minutes. Drain in a colander and transfer to a bowl. Cut away any fat and pull away as much membrane and connective tissue as possible with a small paring knife without breaking up sweetbreads. Mash lightly with a fork while adding the egg, parsley, and flour. Sprinkle with black or white pepper and salt. Heat the oil and shape the fritters with a spoon. Drop them carefully into the hot oil. Fry until golden brown, turning them a couple of times. Place them on a paper towel to drain off excess oil. Serve hot.

Variation: Firmer Fritters

Some cooks prefer to place the sweetbreads in ice water after cooking to make them firmer. They cut the sweetbreads into big pieces, dip each piece in the egg (scrambled), then into flour, and then fry them in the hot oil.

Liver, Italian-Cuban Style

Higado a la Italiana

Serves 4

4 beef liver steaks
½ onion, cut in slices
½ green bell pepper, cut in slices
Salt to taste
3 tbsp. cooking oil (for frying)
Vinegar
Dash black pepper (optional)

Wash the liver steaks and cut them into slices, similar to pepper steak. Place them in a dish with the onions and the green bell peppers. Sprinkle with some salt. Allow them to marinate for a couple of hours before cooking. Heat the oil in a frying pan. Add a few slices of the onions and bell peppers to the oil, and stir a few times. Add the liver with the rest of the onions and bell peppers. Sauté on high heat, turning constantly, until the liver is completely cooked and starts to turn brown. Sprinkle a generous amount of vinegar on top of the liver, and serve immediately. Serve on top of white rice.

Note: Do not add the vinegar when marinating, because it makes the meat tough.

Accompaniments and Side Dishes

White Rice

Arroz Blanco

This rice is the most popular side dish in Cuban cuisine. It is served alone, or with black beans.

Serves 2 to 4

1 cup long grain white rice
1½ cups water
1 tsp. salt
1 tbsp. cooking oil (traditionally
   Cuban: pork lard)

In a small, 2-qt. sauce pot, mix all the ingredients. Bring to a strong boil over high heat, uncovered, then turn the heat to low, stirring until the bubbles subside. Cover and simmer for 15 minutes. When cooking time is up, uncover and fluff with a fork. Serve hot.

White Rice Stuffing

Relleno de Arroz Blanco

Cooked white rice
¼ cup mayonnaise (regular or
   light)
½ cup chopped green onions or
   regular onions
½ cup white wine
Black pepper
Breadcrumbs

Cook the white rice as indicated above. Transfer to a bowl. Add the mayonnaise, chopped onions, wine, and black pepper to taste. Mix completely, and use to stuff roasted tomatoes, baked zucchini, baked acorn squash, or other roasted vegetables. Sprinkle breadcrumbs on top, and broil until the breadcrumbs are golden brown.

Congri

Rice Cooked with Black Beans

To save time, freeze leftover black beans, and use to make *Congri*.

Serves 6 to 8

1 bag dry black beans (14 or 16 oz.)
1 tbsp. salt
¼ lb. bacon slices, cut in 1-inch sections
1 large onion, chopped
5 to 6 large garlic cloves, mashed
1 green bell pepper, chopped
3 cups long grain rice (parboiled)
¼ tsp. cumin powder
¼ tsp. dried oregano leaves, crushed
2 bay leaves
Olive oil

Ten hours before cooking, soak the beans in enough water to cover them by 2 to 3 inches.

In the pressure cooker,* place the beans in enough water to cover them by 2 inches, and add the tbsp. of salt. After the pressure has built, cook for 25 minutes over medium heat. When the pressure is gone, continue to the next step.

Strain the beans and measure 3½ cups of the liquid from the beans. Set aside liquid. Transfer the strained beans to another pot or bowl. The extra liquid may be discarded. In the same cooker (or pot), cook the bacon slices over medium heat until almost crispy. Add the onions, garlic, and green bell pepper. Sauté until onions are transparent. Add the rice and sauté for about 1 minute, scraping the bottom to prevent it from sticking. Add the measured liquid from the beans, the strained beans, and all the spices; you can leave some of the beans out if desired. Check the taste and add more salt if necessary.

Mix everything well and close the pressure cooker. After the pressure has built, cook for 20 minutes over medium heat. Pour 3 to 4 tbsp. of olive oil on the rice when ready to serve. Garnish with pork cracklings or crispy bits of fried bacon.

*Conventional Cooking Method

Soak beans as described above. Using a 5 to 6 qt. Dutch oven or large stockpot, bring the beans to a boil, reduce the heat to medium/high, and partially cover, to allow the steam to escape. Cook for 1½ to 2 hours, or until the beans are tender. Check often, and add more water if necessary. Add the other ingredients as described above. Afterwards, bring the rice and beans to a boil, stirring constantly. Reduce the heat to medium/low, and cook for 30 minutes. Pour the olive oil on the rice when ready to serve. Garnish with pork cracklings or crispy bits of fried bacon.

Congri Oriental

Rice with Red Kidney Beans

The name *Congri Oriental* is given to this *Congri* recipe because it comes from the Cuban province called *Oriente* where they use red kidney beans to cook this rice and beans recipe, instead of traditional black beans.

Serves 6 to 8

1 bag dry red kidney beans (14 or 16 oz.)
1 tbsp. salt
¼ lb. bacon, cut in 1-inch sections
¼ lb. smoked ham, cut into cubes, or smoked ham hocks
1 large onion, chopped
5 to 6 large garlic cloves, mashed
1 green bell pepper, chopped
3 cups long grain rice (parboiled)
¼ tsp. cumin powder
¼ tsp. dried oregano leaves, crushed
2 bay leaves
Olive oil

Ten hours before cooking, soak the beans in enough water to cover them by 2 to 3 inches.

In the pressure cooker,* place the beans in enough water to cover them by 2 inches, and add the tbsp. of salt. If using ham hocks, add them now. After the pressure has built, cook for 25 minutes on medium heat. When the pressure is gone, continue with next step.

Strain the beans, and measure 4½ cups of the liquid from the beans. Set aside liquid. Transfer the strained beans to another pot or bowl. The extra liquid may be discarded. In the same cooker (or pot), cook the bacon slices over medium heat until almost crispy. Add the ham, onions, garlic, and green bell pepper. Sauté until onions are transparent. Add the rice and sauté for about 1 minute, scraping the bottom to prevent it from sticking. Add the measured liquid from the beans and the strained beans; you can leave some of the beans out if desired. Add all the spices. Check the taste, and add more salt if necessary.

Mix everything well, and close the pressure cooker. After the pressure has built, cook for 20 minutes on medium. Pour 3 to 4 tbsp. olive oil on the rice when ready to serve. Garnish with pork cracklings or crispy bits of fried bacon.

*Conventional Cooking Method
Soak the beans as instructed above. Using a 5 to 6 qt. Dutch oven or large stockpot, bring the beans to a boil, reduce the heat to medium/high, and partially cover, to allow the steam to escape. Cook for 1½ to 2 hours or until the beans are tender. Check often, and add more water if necessary. Add all the ingredients as directed above. Afterwards, bring the rice and beans to a boil, stirring constantly. Reduce the heat to medium/low, and cook for 30 minutes. Pour the olive oil on the rice when ready to serve.

Variation: Easy Preparation
You may use canned (in water and salt) red kidney beans for the recipe above. Skip the soaking and the first cooking process of the beans.

Yellow Rice with Ham and Corn

Arroz Amarillo con Jamon

Serves 4

2 tbsp. olive oil
1 small onion, chopped
¼ green bell pepper, chopped
4 to 5 large garlic cloves, mashed
¼ lbs. cooking ham, cut in cubes
   (Can use chorizo instead of ham)
¼ cup white or cooking wine
1 tbsp. tomato paste
1½ cups long grain white rice or
   parboiled rice
2¼ cups water
1 small can kernel corn (8 oz.;
   you can use diced carrots or
   other vegetables in place of
   corn if desired)
1 tsp. salt
Dash cumin powder
Dash oregano
Pinch saffron (for color)

Heat oil in a 2 qt. saucepot. Sauté the onions, green peppers, garlic, and ham until the onions are transparent. Add the wine and tomato paste, and sauté for 1 more minute. Add the rest of the ingredients and heat to a boil again. Stir well, reduce the heat to low, cover, and simmer for 20 minutes.

Temptation Plantains

Platanos Tentacion

Serves 4

3 tbsp. cooking oil
2 very ripe plantains (more black
   spots than yellow)
½ cup cooking wine or dry white
   wine
5 tbsp. sugar (light brown or
   white)
Pinch salt
Sprinkle cinnamon (optional)

Heat oil in a deep skillet; use one that has a lid. Cut the plantains into 4 sections each. Slightly brown the plantains on all sides over medium heat. Add the rest of the ingredients, and stir together. Reduce the heat, and simmer, mostly covered to allow liquids to evaporate, on low until the plantains are very tender and caramelized, approximately 15 minutes.

Fried, Sweet, Ripe Plantains

Platanos Maduros Fritos

Serves 4

2 ripe plantains (yellow with black spots or lines)
Cooking oil for deep frying

Cut the plantains into diagonal slices about ¼-inch thick. Deep fry in hot oil; reduce the fryer to medium/high heat (about 350 degrees) after all plantains, or as many as will fit, are in the oil. Fry until reddish/yellow in color. Drain with skimmer or slotted spoon. Do not place them on paper towels, because they will stick to the towels. It is normal for some slices to get a little burned at the edges.

Fried Green Plantain Patties

Tostones

Serves 4

Cooking oil for deep frying
2 large green plantains, cut into
    1-inch slices
Salt to taste

Fill a deep fryer with 2 to 3 inches of oil, and turn on the heat. Put the plantains in the oil while the oil is still cold. Fry on medium/high heat (350 degrees) until light golden in color. Remove plantains from the oil and place on paper towels. Turn off the heat for now. Using a "Tostonera" (or your fist and brown paper bag), press down on each plantain until it is as flat as a sugar cookie. Reheat oil until very hot, and fry each patty again, turning once, until crispy and golden brown. Remove quickly, and place on paper towels to drain excess oil. Sprinkle them with salt, and serve.

Note: You can garnish the *tostones* with lime juice and mashed garlic.

Mashed Green Plantains

Mofongo

Mofongo is originally from Puerto Rico. However, the cuisines from these two countries have some similarities, and this recipe is one of them.

Serves 4

6 slices bacon (or fried pork cracklings—*chicharrones*)
2 green plantains, cut in 1-inch slices
Cooking oil to deep fry the plantains
6 large garlic cloves, mashed
Dash cumin powder

Fry the bacon slices over medium heat until crispy. Place on paper towels to drain, and crumble. Reserve the fat from the bacon. In a deep fryer, fry the plantains in medium/high heat (350 degrees) until golden in color and tender inside. Remove from heat and place on paper towels to drain off excess oil. Heat the bacon fat and add the garlic cloves. Sauté for about a minute and remove from heat. Do not allow the garlic to burn. Using a large mortar and pestle or large bowl, mash the fried plantains, adding the cumin powder and the garlic with the bacon fat; this gives it flavor and helps soften the mixture. Mix in some of the fried bacon bits and top the *Mofongo* with the rest of the bacon or *chicharrones*.

Note: Chicken broth may be added to help mash the *Mofongo*, if it gets too dry.

Mashed Yellow Plantains

Fufu

Serves 4 to 6

4 yellow plantains
1 tsp. salt
4 to 6 slices bacon or *chicharrones* (fried pork rinds)
6 large garlic cloves, mashed
Dash cumin powder

Peel and cut plantains into 1-inch pieces. Boil in water with the salt until tender, about 20 minutes. Fry bacon slices over medium heat until crispy. Place on paper towels to remove excess fat; crumble into small pieces. Cook the garlic in the bacon fat, being careful not to burn them. Mash the cooked plantains and add the garlic, part of the bacon fat used to cook the garlic, the crumbled bacon, and a dash of cumin powder. Mix everything and place in a serving dish. Garnish with more crispy bacon bits or *chicharrones*.

Malanga Fritters

Frituras de Malanga

This is one of my family's favorite side dishes. I serve it often to dinner guests at their request. It perfectly accompanies all the meat recipes in tomato sauce, such as Beef Stew, Lamb Stew, Oxtail in Spicy Sauce, and others. Malangas should be available in Cuban supermarkets or in supermarkets in areas that have large Cuban populations.

Serves 4

2 large malangas (root vegetable with a brown hairy skin, white creamy meat)
1 egg, beaten
1 tsp. salt or garlic salt
Cooking oil to deep fry

Peel and wash the malangas. Shred them in a vegetable shredder or a hand-held grater. Mix in the beaten egg and the salt; the mixture will have a creamy consistency. Heat oil in a deep skillet or electric fryer. The temperature of the oil should be 350 degrees. Shape the fritters with a tablespoon to look like a flat egg, and drop them into the hot oil. Fry them until golden brown, turning them several times during frying. Place on paper towels when done to drain off excess oil. Serve hot.

Mashed Malanga Roots

Pure de Malanga

Malanga roots have a thicker consistency than potatoes, because their starch content is much higher. They have brown hairy peels and white meat inside.

Serves 2

2 large malanga roots
4 cups chicken broth (salted to taste)
¼ cup whole milk or half-and-half
Olive oil or butter

Peel the malanga roots, and cut them into chunks. In a medium saucepan, bring the chicken broth and the malanga chunks to a boil. Reduce the heat to medium/low, add the milk, and cover. Cook for approximately 25 minutes or until tender. Take out the malangas and place in a serving bowl. Mash them, adding a little of the cooking broth as needed, until the mixture reaches the consistency of mashed potatoes. Pour olive oil or butter on top of the mashed malangas, and mix in lightly with a fork. Save the unused broth for reheating leftovers, because they will harden after a few hours. Serve immediately

Fried Yuccas

Yuca Frita

This recipe is best when using yucca roots that are not overcooked, which makes them too tender.

Serves 4

2 large yucca roots, peeled (boiled in salted water until tender, but firm)
Oil for deep frying
Salt to taste
Lime juice

Prepare the yuccas as indicated in the following Yucca Roots recipe. Refrigerate, and cut them lengthwise to make yucca sticks. Deep fry them in hot oil, until golden brown and crispy. Place on paper towels to drain off excess oil. Sprinkle with salt and lime juice. You can add mashed garlic to the lime juice if you desire.

Yucca Roots with Mojo

Yuca con Mojo

Mojo is a marinade with garlic as the main ingredient. The one used here for the yucca is different from the one used to marinate pork.

Serves 4

Yucca Roots
2 large yucca roots, peeled and cut
   in 3-inch sections
1 tbsp. salt

Mojo
¼ cup cooking oil, pork lard, or fat
   from fried bacon
6 large garlic cloves, mashed
½ small onion, cut in thin slices
Dash cumin powder
Dash oregano
Juice of 1 lime

To prepare the **Yucca Roots,** boil the yucca roots in enough water to cover them. Cook for about 10 minutes. Add the salt and a cup of cold water to the yucca, cover, and continue to cook over medium heat for 30 minutes or until tender.

To make the **Mojo,** heat the oil in a skillet. Add the garlic and onions, and sauté briefly, turning constantly. Do not allow the garlic to turn brown. Transfer the yuccas to a serving platter. Sprinkle with the cumin powder, the oregano, and the lime juice. Pour the hot oil with the garlic and onions over the yuccas, and serve.

Note: The process of adding cold water to the boiling water is called "scaring" the yucca to help make it tender. Though it might seem strange, it seems to work!

Boniatos in Buttery Sauce

Boniatos en Mantequilla

Cuban sweet potatoes have a dark pink peel with white meat inside.

Serves 4

2 tbsp. butter
3 boniatos (Cuban sweet potatoes), peeled and cut into large chunks
4 tbsp. cooking oil
1½ cups water
½ tsp. salt
4 tbsp. sugar
¼ cup milk

In a deep sauce pan (2 qt.), melt the butter and add the rest of the ingredients. Bring to a boil. Reduce the heat to medium/low, and simmer for about 20 minutes or until tender. Keep the pot half-covered while cooking to allow the water to evaporate. Check often to make sure the water does not evaporate before the boniatos are tender. When the water evaporates, the butter and oil should remain in the bottom of the pan. Finish cooking the boniatos in this oil/butter sauce until they are golden in color. Transfer to a serving dish and pour the remaining sauce over them.

Cabbage and Potato Salad

Ensalada de Col y Papas

Serves 4

3 tbsp. olive oil
½ cup sliced or chopped onion
¼ cup green or red bell pepper, chopped or sliced
4 or 5 garlic cloves, mashed
3 tbsp. tomato paste (or 4 tbsp. tomato puree)
2 cups water
1 tsp. salt
Dash black pepper
2 large potatoes, peeled and cut into small chunks
½ cabbage, washed and cut into chunks
Splash vinegar and olive oil

In a deep saucepot, heat the oil. Add the onions, bell peppers, and garlic. Sauté until the onions are transparent. Add the tomato paste, water, and spices, stirring constantly. Add the potatoes and the cabbage. At first, it might seem like the cabbage does not fit, but when it starts to wilt, the cabbage will fit. Check the taste, and add more salt if necessary. Reduce the heat to medium/low, cover, and simmer for about 20 minutes or until the potatoes are tender but firm. Transfer to a serving platter, and splash with vinegar and a generous amount of olive oil. May be served hot or cold. Refrigerate the leftovers; they taste even better the next day.

Fried Cuban Sweet Potatoes

Boniatos Fritos

Cuban sweet potatoes are very sweet and have a dark pink peel with white meat.

Serves 4

3 boniatos (Cuban sweet potatoes)
Bowl salted water
Cooking oil for deep frying

Peel the boniatos and cut them into long wedges. Place them in the bowl of salted water. Soak for 15 to 30 minutes or until you are ready to fry them. This helps prevent the boniatos from becoming discolored after you peel them. Place the boniato wedges in the oil while it is heating; do not wait until it is hot. Fry them in 350 degree oil (medium/high heat) until tender inside and golden brown outside. Use a strainer to remove the boniato wedges from the oil, and place on paper towels to drain off excess oil. Serve immediately.

Sweet Potato Pudding

Pure de Boniato Amarillo

A favorite for Thanksgiving Dinner!

Serves 6 to 8

6 large sweet potatoes, peeled
   and cut into chunks
2 or 3 cinnamon sticks
1 clove, crushed
½ tsp. salt
3 tbsp. butter
½ cup brown sugar
⅓ tsp. allspice
⅛ tsp. ground nutmeg
2 tbsp. cornstarch
½ cup evaporated milk
Cinnamon powder
½ bag marshmallows
¾ cup chopped walnuts (optional)

Boil the sweet potatoes in water with the cinnamon sticks, the clove, and the salt, until tender. Discard the cinnamon sticks and the clove after cooking. Puree the sweet potatoes in a blender and transfer to a large pot. Over medium heat, simmer the puree with the butter, brown sugar, allspice, and nutmeg. Dissolve the cornstarch in the evaporated milk in a separate container. Add this milk and cornstarch mixture to the puree, and simmer until it thickens, turning often. Add the walnuts if desired. Transfer the thickened sweet potato puree to a rectangular glass baking dish. Sprinkle with cinnamon powder, and place the marshmallows on top. Bake in a 350 degree oven until the marshmallows are golden brown, not *burned*.

Red Potato Mash

Pure de Papas Rojas

Serves 6 to 8

5 lbs. red potatoes, washed and cut in chunks
2 garlic cloves
1 tsp. salt
½ cup milk
½ cup butter
½ large cream cheese, softened (regular or ⅓ less fat)
½ cup sour cream (fat free is okay)
Black pepper to taste

Boil potatoes and garlic in salted water, and cook until tender for about 15 minutes. Drain and mash with the milk and the butter. Stir in cream cheese, sour cream, and pepper.

Sliced Golden Potatoes and Onions

Ruedas de Papas y Cebollas

A great recipe to accompany salmon, steak, and other grilled meats.

Serves 4

4 tbsp. cooking oil
2 large Idaho potatoes, cut in thin slices (¼ inch)
½ red onion, cut in slices
Salt to taste
Black pepper to taste
¾ cup water

There is no need to peel the potatoes. Heat the oil in a large, deep skillet. Arrange the potatoes in a domino-like row all around the skillet—in a spiral toward the center—until they cover the entire bottom. Lightly brown the potatoes on both sides. Add the onions and sauté everything a little more, while adding the salt and the black pepper. Add ¾ cup of water, reduce the heat, and simmer, half covered, for about 10 minutes or until the potatoes are tender and the water has evaporated.

Chickpea Stew
Cocido de Garbanzo

Serves 4 to 6

1 bag (14 oz. to 16 oz.) dry garbanzo beans (chickpeas)
1 tbsp. salt
1 large potato, peeled and cut into small chunks
3 tbsp. olive oil
1 large onion, chopped
½ cup green/red bell peppers, chopped
5 to 6 large garlic cloves, mashed
2 Spanish sausages (chorizo), cut into thick slices
¼ cup tomato paste
¼ cup red/cooking wine
Dash paprika
¼ tsp. cumin powder
Dash oregano
Dash black pepper
Salt to taste
Dash crushed red pepper
Splash vinegar and olive oil

Soak the dry beans overnight, or for 10 hours, in enough water to cover the beans by 2 inches. After soaking, cook for 40 minutes in the pressure cooker,* with the water used for soaking the beans, plus enough water to cover the beans by 2 inches, and 1 tbsp. of salt. Start timing after the pressure has built, and reduce the heat to medium. When the beans are finished cooking and the pressure is gone, open the pressure cooker and strain the liquid out.

Reserve about 4 cups of the broth from the beans, and pour in a smaller pot. Cook the potato chunks in this broth for about 15 minutes, or until tender. Freeze the rest of the liquid for later use in soups. In the meantime, heat the olive oil in a medium-sized pot. Add the onions, bell peppers, garlic, and Spanish sausages. Sauté until onions are translucent. Add the tomato paste and the cooking wine, stir gently to combine everything, and lower the heat. Add the cooked potatoes and the rest of the dry ingredients (spices), and stir together, being careful not to break the potatoes, nor the beans. Check the taste, and add more salt if necessary. Cover and simmer everything over medium/low heat for 10 to 15 minutes. If it becomes too dry, add a little more wine. Splash with vinegar and olive oil before serving. This dish is very tasty, and on the dry side, with a thick tomato sauce. Serve as a side dish for meats.

*Conventional Cooking Method
Use a large Dutch oven or large stockpot to cook the chickpeas in enough water to cover them by 3 inches for 1½ hours, or until tender. Continue with the recipe above, beginning with the potatoes in broth.

Munyeta

Mashed White Beans

Serves 6 to 8

1 bag (14 or 16 oz.) navy beans
  (white beans)
4 cups water with 2 tsp. salt added
4 tbsp. olive oil
1 medium onion, finely chopped
  or put through a food processor
¼ green bell pepper, finely
  chopped or put through a
  food processor
5 cloves of garlic, mashed
¼ lb. salted pork, cubed or bacon
1 chorizo (Spanish sausage), cut
  into thick slices
¼ lb. cooking ham, cubed
¼ cup tomato puree or paste
Dash cumin powder
Dash black pepper

Soak beans in water for about 10 hours, or overnight.

In a large stockpot or Dutch oven, cook the beans in salted wa-ter for 1½ to 2 hours, or until tender. Drain and mash the beans.

Heat olive oil in a deep frying pan. Add the onions, green peppers, garlic, salted pork, chorizo, and ham, and sauté for a couple of minutes. Add tomato puree and keep turning. Slowly add beans, turning and mixing evenly. Add more salt to taste, pepper, and cumin powder and cook until the mixture is very thick and almost turning brown in color. Serve hot as a side dish for meats. May also be served as a dip with chips.

Note: You can also use canned beans in water and salt.

Quick Green Bean Casserole

Caserola de Habichuelas Verdes

Serves 4

1 lb. green beans, steamed (bought frozen or fresh)
1 egg, beaten
1 can cream of mushroom soup (10¾ oz.)
2 tbsp. butter
½ cup breadcrumbs
½ cup sliced almonds

Cook green beans according to package directions. Drain, and mix in beaten egg and the can of mushroom soup. Transfer to a glass casserole dish. In a skillet, melt the butter and add about ½ cup of breadcrumbs. Toast the breadcrumbs until golden brown, turning often. Toast the almonds by placing them in one layer on a cookie sheet, and broiling them until golden brown. Mix half of the almonds into the green bean mixture. Top the green beans with the rest of the toasted almonds and the breadcrumbs, and bake in a 350 degree oven for about 25 minutes.

Note: Double the recipe if using a large "family size" bag of green beans.

Tabbouleh Salad

This is traditionally paired with Kibbe, found in the Pork, Beef, and Other Meats section. Both recipes reflect the strong influence of the Lebanese population in Cuba.

Serves 6

¾ cup cracked wheat (bulgur)
3 cups fresh, ripe tomatoes, cubed
½ cup green onions, chopped
1 cup parsley, chopped
½ cup mint leaves, chopped
½ tsp. allspice
½ tsp. salt
Black pepper to taste
1 cup chopped cucumbers (optional)
½ cup olive oil
½ cup lemon juice

Soak the bulgur in warm water for 1 hour; use enough water to cover the wheat by 1 inch. Drain completely. Combine all the ingredients except for the oil and lemon juice. Chill until dinner time. Mix in the olive oil and lemon right before serving, and toss well.

Fettuccine with Tomato Cream Sauce

Pasta Fettuccine con Salsa de Tomate

Serves 4 to 6

1 box fettuccine pasta (16 oz.)
3 tbsp. butter
4 garlic cloves, mashed
1 lb. shrimp, peeled and cleaned,
   or scallops (optional)
½ tsp. salt
Dash crushed red pepper
Dash black pepper
Pinch thyme
Bunch fresh parsley, chopped
   (do not use the long stems)
2 cups fresh or canned tomatoes
⅔ cup heavy cream

Boil the pasta according to directions. In deep sauce pan, melt the butter and add the garlic, the shrimp or scallops if desired, and spices; sauté for 2 minutes. Add the tomatoes and the cream, and simmer for a few minutes, stirring constantly. Serve over the fettuccine.

Fettuccine Alfredo

This is one of the easiest recipes I can recommend to the beginner cook. Serve alone or with the simple Spanish (and universal) favorite Garlic Shrimp (found in the Seafood section) on top.

Serves 4 to 6

1 box fettuccine pasta (16 oz.)
4 tbsp. unsalted butter
1 cup heavy cream
1 egg yolk
Dash pepper
¾ cup grated Parmesan cheese (Reggiano or other good quality)

Boil the pasta, following instructions on the box. In a small sauce pan, melt the butter. Slowly, add the cup of heavy cream, stirring constantly. Add the egg yolk, pepper, and parmesan cheese. Keep stirring for a few minutes until sauce thickens. Strain the pasta of excess water, and transfer to a large serving bowl. Pour the sauce over the pasta and stir to cover completely.

Soft Polenta
Polenta Estilo Italiano

Serves 4

5 cups water
1 cup yellow or white cornmeal
2 tsp. salt
3 tbsp. unsalted butter
⅛ tsp. black pepper, freshly ground
½ cup gorgonzola cheese or mozzarella cheese

Combine water, cornmeal, and salt in a 2 qt. microwave-safe glass container. Cook, uncovered, for 6 minutes in the microwave. Stir well, cover loosely with paper towel, and cook for 6 minutes more. Remove from microwave. Stir in butter, black pepper, and cheese or additional butter. Let stand for 3 minutes. Serve hot.

Desserts

Best Flan

Best Egg Custard

This is a very special *flan*. Typically, the *flan* is not made with cream cheese, but after trying this recipe, everyone agrees it is the best they have ever tasted!

Serves 8 to 10

Caramelized Top
2 cups sugar
¼ cup water

Flan
1 can evaporated milk (12 oz.)
1 can condensed milk (14 oz.)
5 eggs
¼ 8-oz. cream cheese (regular or Neufchatel), cut into 3 pieces
5 tbsp. sugar
2 tbsp. vanilla extract

To prepare the **Caramelized Top,** put the 2 cups of sugar with about ¼ cup of water in a small sauce pan. Wet the sugar completely. Cook over medium/high heat until the syrup is reduced and the color turns "bronze," being careful not to let it burn. At this point, remove quickly from heat and move the pan carefully, turning it slowly to stop the cooking process. You will notice that it continues to cook even after it is removed from the heat. Transfer the syrup to a deep, round pan that will fit in the pressure cooker. A Bundt cake pan works perfectly. Turn the pan to cover the sides with the caramelized syrup. Allow to cool, then chill for a few minutes.

To prepare the **Flan,** place all the other ingredients in a blender, and process at a low speed until completely mixed. Wait until the foam subsides, or try to break the bubbles with a wooden spoon as much as possible. This foam will become a spongy layer when the flan is cooked. Pour the mix slowly into the caramelized pan. In the pressure cooker,* pour about 1 inch of water. Place the pan inside the cooker, and close. Wait for the pressure to build, and cook for exactly 18 minutes. When time is up, place the cooker in the sink at once, and pour cool water on it until the pressure is gone. Open and remove the flan from the cooker to avoid overcooking.

Let flan cool and place it in the refrigerator for at least 6 hours, or overnight. When it is completely chilled, cover the flan with a round glass pie pan (or quiche pan) and turn the flan over. Serve cold, and keep refrigerated.

*Conventional Cooking Method
Place the pan or 8" by 8" glass dish with the flan mixture inside a larger rectangular baking dish. Pour an inch of water into the larger pan, and place in the oven. Bake at 350 degrees for 1 hour. Remove the pan with the flan from the hot water, to avoid overcooking. Cool and refrigerate as directed above.

Diplomatic Pudding

Pudin Diplomatico

According to cooking lore, Diplomatic Pudding was first served at a diplomatic conference in the early twentieth century. The guests liked it so much, the chef published the recipe. However, not everyone agrees with that theory. Other accounts credit it to a famous Russian diplomat who loved English puddings.

Serves 16 to 18

Caramelized Glaze
2 cups sugar
½ cup water

Pudding
2 cups milk or 1 cup evaporated and 1 cup whole milk
2 cinnamon sticks
½ tsp. grated lime peel
1 can condensed milk (14 oz.)
6 eggs
1 cup sugar
Dash salt
4 tbsp. apricot brandy (or Grand Marnier, Amaretto, or Galliano)
1 tbsp. vanilla extract
1½ cups fruit cocktail, strained
1 pound cake (or white bread slices)
¼ cup melted butter
¼ cream cheese or Neufchatel

To prepare the **Caramelized Glaze,** boil the water with the sugar over medium heat until it turns golden-bronze in color. Remove from heat, and pour syrup into the baking dish that will be used to bake the pudding. Turn the dish carefully to coat the entire bottom with the caramel. Let cool. Proceed with the rest of the recipe below.

To prepare the **Pudding,** boil the 2 cups of milk with the cinnamon sticks and the lime peel for about 2 minutes. Let cool and strain. In a blender, mix the condensed milk, eggs, sugar, salt, 2 tbsp. brandy, and vanilla. Add the strained milk, and blend on the lowest setting. Pour this mixture into the dish with the caramelized glaze. On top of the mixture, place the strained fruits to cover the entire top. Peel the top "skin" from the pound cake—to show the spongy cake only—and cut into ¼-inch slices. If using white bread, remove the crust all around the slices. Brush every slice with the rest of the brandy and the melted butter. Cover the entire top of the pudding with the slices, placing them on top of the fruits. Brush the top of the slices with more melted butter.

Place the dish with the pudding inside a larger rectangular pan with approximately 1 inch of water, using the double boiler method. Bake in 350 degree oven for about 1 hour. Chill completely for about 6 hours before turning it over on a serving dish. Serving dish should have sides of at least 1 inch to hold the syrup. Keep refrigerated. The brandy taste improves as the days go by!

Pumpkin Custard

Flan de Calabaza

Even though the name says Custard or *flan*, this recipe is cooked like a pudding.

Serves 8 to 10

Glaze
2 cups sugar
½ cup water

Pumpkin Custard
1½ lbs. Cuban-style pumpkin (calabaza), peeled and cut into chunks
1 tsp. salt
1 can condensed milk (14 oz.)
Cinnamon sticks and powder
Dash ground nutmeg
5 heaping tbsp. cornstarch
1 can evaporated milk (12 oz.)
1 tbsp. vanilla extract

To prepare the **Glaze,** boil the 2 cups of sugar in ½ cup of water, moistening the sugar completely with the water, over medium heat until it is golden brown. Once it has reached the perfect color, transfer it at once to the mold you will be using to chill the custard. Turn the mold several times to coat the entire bottom and some of the sides.

To prepare the **Pumpkin Custard,** cook the pumpkin in water and salt until tender. Puree in a blender, and transfer to a large pot. Add the condensed milk, 2 or 3 cinnamon sticks, and nutmeg. In a separate container, dilute the cornstarch in the evaporated milk and strain it while you add it to the pumpkin puree. Cook this mixture over medium heat, turning often with a wooden spoon or spatula. When the custard thickens and it sticks to a spoon inserted into it, remove from the heat, and add the vanilla while turning it. Pour it into the mold that has been glazed, and sprinkle with cinnamon powder. Chill for a few hours, or overnight, until firm. Carefully turn upside down into a glass serving dish—pie or quiche pans work well—by covering with the glass pan and turning it over while holding both the mold and serving dish tightly.

Heaven Custard

Tocinillo del Cielo

This is a very sweet and rich dessert. It is originally from Spain, but it has been adopted by Cubans as one of their own.

Serves 8 to 10

Caramel Glaze
½ cup water
2 cups sugar

Heaven Custard
¾ cup water
1¾ cups sugar
5 drops lime juice
½ cup egg yolks
½ cup whole eggs (a total of about 9 eggs)
1 tbsp. vanilla extract

To prepare the **Caramel Glaze,** combine the water and sugar in a small 1 qt. pot, and boil over medium heat until the syrup turns golden-bronze. Pour the syrup into the mold that will be used for the custard. Use a glass or metal mold with 2 inch or more sides. Turn the mold several times to coat the entire bottom, as well as part of the sides.

To prepare the **Heaven Custard,** boil the water with the sugar and the lime juice over medium heat until it is reduced to 1 cup of syrup. Allow it to cool. Beat the egg yolks with the whole eggs until blended. Add the sugar syrup and the vanilla, and blend completely. Strain the mixture, and pour into the mold with the **Caramel Glaze**. Place inside a larger pan with about 1 inch of water. Bake in a 350 degree oven for approximately 1 hour and 15 minutes.

Spanish Crème Brulee

Crema Catalana o Natilla

Serves 6

2½ cups milk or 1½ cups milk
   and 1 cup evaporated milk
1 can condensed milk (14 oz.)
2 cinnamon sticks
½ tsp. grated lemon rind
2 heaping tbsp. cornstarch
6 egg yolks
1 or 2 tbsp. vanilla extract
6 tbsp. brown sugar for glazing

I strongly recommend cooking this pudding in a double boiler pot. If not available, use only medium/low heat. Heat 1½ cups of milk, the can of condensed milk, cinnamon sticks, and lemon rind over medium heat. Dissolve the 2 tbsp. of cornstarch in about ¼ cup of water or milk until there are no lumps; you may strain it for smoother texture. Beat the egg yolks with the other cup of milk, and add the dissolved cornstarch to this. Add this mixture to the heated milk in the pot while turning with a wooden spoon or spatula. Keep cooking over medium heat, while turning, until the pudding thickens. At this point, add the vanilla extract, remove the cinnamon sticks, and pour into 6 individual bowls. Chill until set. Sprinkle each bowl with 1 tbsp. of brown sugar and ignite with a kitchen torch until sugar is melted and caramelized. Serve chilled.

Note: My recipe for Vanilla Pudding (*Natilla*) is the same, except it does not call for glazed sugar on top nor grated lemon rind.

Three Milks

Tres Leches

Serves 16 to 18

Three Milks

1 18-oz. box yellow cake mix (3 extra eggs and vegetable oil or any other ingredients the cake directions call for)
1 can evaporated milk (12 oz.)
1 can condensed milk (14 oz.)
1¼ cups whole milk or half-and-half
3 egg yolks (reserve the whites in a dry bowl)
3 tbsp. sugar
1 tbsp. vanilla extract
Maraschino cherries

Heavy Syrup

¾ cup sugar
⅓ bottle Karo light corn syrup (16 oz. bottle)

To make the **Three Milks,** bake cake according to directions on the box. Bake in a 9"x 13" glass baking dish. Let cool, and carefully remove the thin brown layer formed on top of the cake. This will show the sponge-like cake. In a blender, mix the rest of the ingredients, except the cherries, until smooth. Pour the mix over the cake slowly, allowing it to be soaked into the cake. Cool in refrigerator.

To prepare the **Heavy Syrup,** mix the sugar into the syrup in a small pot. Boil only until the sugar is diluted and clear. Do *not* overcook. Let the syrup cool. It will feel a little heavy when stirring it as it cools.

In the meantime, make a meringue by beating the reserved egg whites with a mixer until stiff. Without stopping the mixer, sweeten the meringue with the **Heavy Syrup.** Keep mixing until well blended and shiny. Spread the meringue on the cake and decorate with maraschino cherries.

Variation: Cinnamon Flavor

Boil the whole milk with 2 cinnamon sticks for 2 minutes. Let cool, and remove the sticks before adding to the blender. Skip the vanilla extract when using this variation.

Rum Cake

Cake de Ron

Cake
1 box "pudding in the mix" yellow cake mix

3 eggs

½ cup dark rum (gold or Añejo)

⅓ cup cooking oil

½ cup water

¼ cup light brown (or brown) sugar, mixed with ½ tsp. cinnamon powder

1 cup chopped pecans (walnuts or sliced almonds may also be used)

Glaze
1 stick butter (8 tbsp.)

1 cup light brown (or brown) sugar

¼ cup water

½ cup dark rum (more if desired)

To prepare the **Cake,** preheat oven to 325 degrees. In a mixer with a large bowl, place all the cake ingredients, except for the brown sugar and the pecans. Grease the bottom and sides of a Bundt cake pan; oil spray may be used on the pan. Sprinkle the bottom of the pan with the nuts. Add the brown sugar mixture over the nuts. Pour the cake batter over this, and bake for 50 minutes, or until a knife inserted in the cake comes out clean. Allow to cool completely, and invert on a serving dish.

In the meantime prepare the **Glaze.** Melt the butter in a small saucepan. Add the sugar and the water, and stir to dissolve. Boil for 3 minutes. Remove from heat, and add the rum. Stir to mix in. Glaze the cake by pouring the syrup slowly over the top and sides of the cake, allowing it to be absorbed.

Note: If using sliced almonds instead of pecans, use ½ cup of any almond liqueur (such as Amaretto) instead of the dark rum for the cake.

"Drunken" Sponge Cake

Panetela Borracha

Serves 12 to 14

Sponge Cake
6 eggs, separated
1 cup sugar
1 cup flour, sifted
1½ tsp. baking powder
1 tbsp. vanilla extract
Sugar/rum syrup (recipe below)

Sugar Syrup
1 cup water
1 tsp. Spanish anise seeds
2 cups sugar
¼ cup light rum or dry cooking
    wine

To prepare the **Sponge Cake,** preheat the oven to 325 degrees. Beat the egg yolks with the sugar until very light in color. Mix the flour and baking powder together and add to the egg yolks. Mix in the vanilla. In a separate bowl, beat the egg whites until they form stiff peaks. Gently fold egg whites into the egg yolk batter with a wooden or rubber spatula, and pour into a greased, 9" by 13" glass baking pan. Bake for 20 to 25 minutes, until a knife inserted in the center comes out clean.

To prepare the **Sugar Syrup,** boil the water with the anise seeds for 2 minutes. You should have about ¾ cup of water left. Strain and discard the seeds. Add the sugar to that water, and boil for approximately 3 minutes. Remove from heat, add the light rum, and stir to mix well.

Pour the sugar/rum syrup on the cake, poking it with a fork to help it absorb all the syrup. Serve cold.

Note: Can be topped with vanilla pudding and decorated with peach or pear slices, as shown in the picture.

Baklavah

This Baklavah recipe comes from Lebanon. The Lebanese community was influential in Cuba, leaving us with some amazing dishes. It is a little time consuming, but well worth the effort!

Serves 15 (2 pieces per person)

3 cups chopped walnuts
¾ cup sugar
1 tbsp. water
1 tbsp. vanilla
1 pound frozen phyllo dough
　(about 20 17" x 12" sheets)
1½ cups butter, melted
1½ cups water
1 cup sugar
3 tbsp. lemon juice

In a bowl stir together the walnuts, ¾ cup of sugar, 1 tbsp. of water and the vanilla; set aside. Cut phyllo sheets to fit the bottom of a 13 x 9 x 2 inch baking pan. First brush the pan with some of the melted butter; layer half of the phyllo sheets in the glass pan, carefully brushing every two sheets with some of the melted butter. Spoon the walnut mixture on top, and drizzle with some more of the melted butter. Layer the rest of the phyllo sheets one or two at a time, brushing each with melted butter. With a sharp knife, cut the Baklavah into small diamond-shaped pieces. Drizzle remaining melted butter on top. Bake in a 325 degree oven for 60 minutes or until golden brown. In a saucepan combine the remaining 1½ cups of water and the 1 cup of sugar. Bring to a boil, then lower the heat, and simmer for 10 minutes. Stir in lemon juice. Cool and pour the syrup over the hot baked pastry. Cool completely on wire rack.

Walnut and Sugar Pastries

Empanadillas de nueces, azucaradas

This is a recipe brought to Cuba from the Lebanese community, which introduced Cuba to some great tasting recipes.

Serves 12

Pastries
6 tbsp. milk
3 tbsp. cooking oil
¼ tsp. salt
12 tbsp. flour
2 cups chopped walnuts
⅓ cup sugar (Light brown works
    better)

Heavy Syrup
2 cups sugar
½ cup water

To prepare the **Pastries,** mix the milk, oil, and salt in a large bowl. Add the flour a little at a time, blending completely, but do not knead. Cover with plastic wrap, and let stand for 30 minutes. During this time, mash the chopped walnuts and mix with the sugar in a bowl. Unwrap the dough, and knead well to form a roll. Cut into 2-inch sections, and roll out each section with a rolling pin, forming 4-inch-wide flat disks. Fill each one with a tbsp. of the walnut/sugar mixture in the center. Wet the outside edge, and fold, pressing down with a fork to seal. Deep fry in hot oil.

Meanwhile, to prepare the **Heavy Syrup,** boil the sugar with the water for several minutes until it has thickened and reduced. Place in a bowl to dip the pastries when fried.

As you take the pastries out of the oil, dip them briefly in the heavy sugar syrup. Allow to coat, and take them out, placing them on a serving tray or plate.

Bread Pudding

Pudin de Pan

You haven't found a more amazing Bread Pudding than this one! The Rum Sauce is a fabulous extra touch.

Serves about 18

Bread Pudding
1 loaf French or Cuban bread, cut into cubes
3 cups milk
3 eggs
1 can condensed milk (14 oz.)
1 cup sugar
2 tbsp. vanilla extract
1 tsp. cinnamon powder
1 cup pitted prunes
3 tbsp. unsalted butter

Rum Sauce
1 stick butter
1½ cups brown sugar
⅓ cup dark rum (or ½ cup if desired)

To prepare the **Bread Pudding,** place the bread cubes and the milk in a large bowl, allowing them to soak. Cover with plastic wrap and let stand for 1 hour. Beat the eggs with the condensed milk, sugar, vanilla, and cinnamon, and add to the bread, mixing everything well. Fold in the prunes as well. Melt the butter in a 9" by 13" glass baking pan. Turn the pan to coat the bottom and sides completely. Pour the bread/milk mixture into the pan, and bake at 375 degrees for 1 hour.

To prepare the **Rum Sauce,** melt the butter in a small sauce pan over medium heat. Add the sugar and simmer until dissolved and bubbling. Remove from heat and add the rum. Pour over the hot pudding immediately, and poke pudding with a fork to allow it to soak through.

Corn Pudding

Majarete

This recipe calls for a very specialized ingredient available in the U.S. only in cities where there is a large Cuban population. "Ground, young, tender corn" is sold in natural fruit stores (fruterias).

Serves 8 to 10

2 lbs. ground, young, tender corn
  (*maiz tierno*)
1 can evaporated milk (12 oz.)
1 can condensed milk (14 oz.)
½ cup sugar
½ tsp. salt
2 or 3 cinnamon sticks
Dash ground nutmeg
1 tbsp. vanilla extract
Cinnamon powder

Pour 1 cup of the ground corn with 3 cups of water into a blender, and blend until smooth. Strain this mixture, and pour it into a large (6 or 8 qt.) pot. Put the pulp left in the strainer back in the blender with 1 cup of water, and blend again until smooth. Strain and pour it in the pot. Repeat this process as long as the strained liquid is "milky." Do this process until you are finished with the entire 2 lbs. of corn. (I know—it's a lot of work!)

Cook the strained "milky" corn over medium heat, adding the rest of the ingredients, except for the vanilla and the cinnamon powder. Cook for approximately 1 hour or until the pudding thickens, stirring often. When it is done, remove from heat and add the vanilla extract. Pour into small serving bowls or a large serving dish, and sprinkle with cinnamon powder. Serve chilled.

Cornmeal Pudding
Dulce de Harina

Serves 8 to 10

1 cup cornmeal, fine or coarse
5 cups water
2 or 3 cinnamon sticks
2 tbsp. butter
½ tsp. salt
1 can evaporated milk (12 oz.)
1 can condensed milk (14 oz.)
1 cup sugar
¾ cup raisins or prunes
Dash ground nutmeg
1 tbsp. vanilla extract
Cinnamon powder

Cook the cornmeal in the 5 cups of water with the cinnamon sticks, butter, and salt. Bring water to a boil, cover, and simmer over medium/low heat for approximately 25 minutes. Uncover pan and add the 2 cans of milk, sugar, raisins, and nutmeg. Simmer over low heat for about 1 hour, stirring often to prevent it from sticking. When the pudding is reduced and thick, remove from heat and add the vanilla extract. Pour into a glass serving dish, and sprinkle with cinnamon powder. It can also be poured into individual serving bowls. Serve chilled.

Note: I prefer to eat mine warm. When it is cold, the pudding becomes hard and has to be cut with a knife, much like bread pudding.

Rice Pudding

Arroz con Leche

Serves 8 to 10

Rice Pudding
1 cup Valencia style rice (short grain)
5 cups water
3 cinnamon sticks
¼ tsp. salt
1 can evaporated milk (12 oz.)
1 can condensed milk (14 oz.)
1 cup sugar
2 tbsp. vanilla extract
Cinnamon powder

Cinnamon and Anise Tea
1 cup water
2 or 3 cinnamon sticks
1 tsp. anise seeds

To prepare the **Rice Pudding,** soak the rice in the 5 cups of water for a few hours. In a large 6 qt. Dutch oven, boil the 5 cups of water with the rice, cinnamon sticks, and salt for about 1 minute. Reduce the heat to low, and cook, covered, for about 25 minutes, stirring occasionally.

To prepare the **Cinnamon and Anise Tea,** boil the water, cinnamon sticks, and anise seeds in a small sauce pan for 2 minutes. Strain and set aside.

After the **Rice Pudding** has cooked for 25 minutes, uncover the rice, and add the cinnamon and anise tea, the 2 cans of milk, and the sugar. Simmer over medium/low heat, slowly stirring very often to avoid sticking. Cook, uncovered, for about 45 minutes, or until the sauce is thick and somewhat reduced. Remove from heat, and add the vanilla extract, mixing it in slowly. Be careful not to scrape the bottom of the pan. Transfer to a glass serving bowl, and sprinkle with cinnamon powder.

Sweet Milk Dessert

Dulce de Leche Cortada

This is a very rich sweet milk dessert. The many eggs used in this recipe make it especially creamy.

Serves 6 to 8

12 cups milk
9 eggs
5 cups sugar
4 cinnamon sticks
2 tbsp. vanilla extract
Juice from 1 lime

Blend 2 cups of milk with the eggs. In a large sauce pot, heat the other 10 cups of milk with the sugar. With the heat on high, pour the egg mixture into the pot and add the cinnamon sticks, vanilla, and the lime juice, stirring well. When it comes to a boil and the milk looks like it is getting curdled, turn off the heat and wait until the foam subsides and it settles down. Turn on the heat again to medium/low and cook, uncovered, for about 1½ hours, stirring occasionally around the sides and the bottom of the pot. Be careful not to disturb the milk too much when stirring. Transfer to a serving bowl and serve chilled.

Easy Sweet Milk Dessert

Dulce de Leche Facil

Serves 5 to 6

2 cups milk
1 can evaporated milk (12 oz.)
1¼ cups sugar
2 eggs, beaten
1 tbsp. vanilla extract
3 cinnamon sticks
¼ cup lime juice

In a large pot, heat the milk with the sugar, the eggs, the vanilla, and the cinnamon sticks. Add the lime juice, mix well, and bring the milk to a boil. When the milk curdles, reduce the heat to low and cook, uncovered, for about 1 hour stirring occasionally through the sides and the bottom of the pot. Be careful not to disturb the milk too much when stirring. When it is reduced and the syrup is caramel colored, remove from the heat and transfer to a serving bowl. Serve chilled or warm.

Tiramisu

Serves 15

1 box yellow cake mix (pudding in the mix type; 18 oz. box)

3 cups milk

4 tbsp. sugar

3 cinnamon sticks

¾ tsp. ground nutmeg

8 tbsp. cocoa powder

12 tbsp. coffee liqueur (Kahlua, Tia Maria, etc.)

5 egg yolks

6 tbsp. powdered sugar

1 lb. Mascarpone cheese (or ½ lb. Ricotta and ½ lb. cream cheese)

1 oz. hard dark chocolate for cooking, grated

Make the yellow cake according to directions on the box. Make sure you grease and flour the pan for easy removal of the cake. Bake in a 9"by 13" glass baking pan. Allow to cool for a few minutes. Boil the milk with the 4 tbsp. of sugar, the cinnamon sticks, and the nutmeg for about 2 minutes. Separately, dissolve 3 tbsp. of the cocoa powder in the coffee liqueur. Add this mixture to the milk, blending it well; chill. With a mixer, beat the egg yolks with the powdered sugar until it forms a thick foam. Add the Mascarpone cheese and mix some more.

Carefully take the cake out of the baking pan. Remove the top, brown layer of the cake, and with a long bread knife, cut the cake lengthwise into 2 rectangular layers. The layers must be thin. Place one layer of the cake back into the 9" by 13" baking pan. Pour half of the milk/liqueur mix on the cake layer, poking the cake with a fork to help it absorb the milk. Spread half of the Mascarpone and egg mixture evenly on top of this layer, and sprinkle with 1 tbsp. of cocoa powder. Sprinkle half of the grated dark chocolate on the mixture, and place the other half of the cake on top, pressing lightly. Repeat the layering of the milk and liqueur, cheese and egg, chocolate, and the rest of the cocoa powder to finish. Serve well chilled.

Orange Pudding

Natilla De Naranja

Serves 8

4 navel oranges plus enough orange juice to total 4 cups
4 to 5 tbsp. sugar
2 heaping tbsp. cornstarch
¾ cup milk
1 egg yolk (reserve egg white)
3 to 4 tbsp. sugar

Cut each orange in half, and extract the juice from each one using a juicer. Do not damage the peel. Carefully remove the inside of the orange, reserving the intact peel for later. In a medium sauce pan, heat the 4 cups of orange juice with 4 to 5 tbsp. of sugar. Dissolve the cornstarch in the milk and mix in the egg yolk. Pour this mixture into the pot with the orange juice. Simmer over medium/low heat, stirring constantly with a wooden spoon, until it thickens.

Meanwhile, beat the reserved egg white until it forms a peak. Add 3 to 4 tablespoons of sugar and continue beating until shiny, forming a meringue.

Serve pudding in the half oranges, and decorate with a scoop of meringue on top. Chill until set before serving.

Note: You can cut the rims of the oranges with peaks or other designs for a fancy presentation.

Pudding-Stuffed Chayotes

Chayotes Rellenos

This is a very old-fashioned Cuban recipe, dating back to my grandmother's generation. Chayotes are also known as vegetable pears or mirlitons.

Serves 6 to 8

4 chayotes
½ tsp. salt
4 eggs
1 can evaporated milk (12 oz.)
1¼ cups sugar
3 heaping tbsp. cornstarch
¼ cup milk
2 cinnamon sticks
¾ cup raisins
¼ cup sliced almonds
1 tbsp. vanilla extract
2 to 3 tbsp. butter
4 tbsp. cracker meal or fine breadcrumbs

The shells from the chayotes will be used as cups to serve the pudding. Do not peel them and handle them gently. Cut the chayotes in half lengthwise and boil in water with the ½ tsp. of salt until almost tender. Drain, and scoop out the flesh with a plastic spoon, being careful not to cut through the peel.

In a blender, puree the chayote flesh with the eggs, evaporated milk, and sugar. Transfer the puree to a medium-sized saucepot and turn the heat to medium. Dissolve the cornstarch in milk, strain, and pour into the chayote mixture. Add the cinnamon sticks and cook over medium heat, stirring often with a wooden spoon, until the pudding thickens. Reduce the heat to low and add the raisins and sliced almonds, stirring slowly until mixed. Discard the cinnamon sticks. Simmer for a few more minutes and remove from heat. Add the vanilla extract and stir to mix. Transfer to a large bowl and chill until set.

Meanwhile, melt the butter in a skillet and add the cracker meal. Cook, scraping the bottom of the skillet often, until golden brown.

Spoon the chilled pudding into the chayote shells. Fill them all the way up, rounding them above the rims. Cover the top with the toasted cracker meal.

Yucca Doughnut Fritter

Buñuelos

This is an old-fashioned Cuban favorite. It is the traditional dessert served on Christmas Eve.

Serves 8 (makes many *buñuelos*)

Buñuelos
3 large yucca roots, peeled and cut into chunks
½ tsp. salt
2 tbsp. butter
1 egg
2 tbsp. sugar
½ cup flour (more if necessary)
¼ to ½ tsp. Spanish anise seeds, crushed
Cooking oil to deep fry

Sugar Syrup
¾ cup water
1 tsp. anise seeds
2 cups sugar

To prepare the **Buñuelos,** boil the yucca root chunks with the salt in enough water to cover them. Reduce the heat, and simmer over medium/low heat until tender. Drain well and mash with the butter in a large bowl. Add the egg, sugar, flour, and anise seeds. Mix everything and roll a piece between your hands to form a long thin roll, about ½ inch by 8 or 10 inches, that will be shaped into a figure-8. Use more flour if the dough is too sticky. Deep fry them in hot oil until golden brown.

To prepare the **Sugar Syrup,** boil the water with the anise seeds for 3 minutes. Strain the water, discard the seeds, and add 2 cups of sugar. Bring to a boil and cook for about 2 minutes. For thicker syrup, add more sugar before cooking.

After draining excess oil from the *buñuelos* with paper towels, place them in a serving bowl, and pour the sugar syrup on top.

Note: If you do not like to find anise seeds when eating the *buñuelos*, boil ½ cup of water with the anise seeds for 3 minutes, strain, and use that water when mashing the yucca.

Variation: Combination Doughnut Fritters
In different parts of Cuba, the *buñuelos* are made from 4 different root vegetables in equal parts: 1 yucca, 1 malanga, 1 boniato, and 1 ñame. Instead of sugar syrup, they are served with molasses.

Churros

Traditional Cuban "Doughnuts"

This special treat came to Cuba from Spain, where it is traditionally served with hot chocolate.

Yields 14 to 16 *churros*

½ cup water
½ cup milk
2 tbsp. butter
½ tsp. salt
1 cup all purpose flour
Cooking oil for deep frying
½ cup sugar

In a medium saucepan, heat the water and milk with the butter and salt. When it starts to boil, add the flour all at once and beat quickly with a wooden spoon until the mixture forms a ball. The mixture will be very sticky. Use a good quality *churros* or pastry press fitted with a star shaped tip. Fill with the dough, and squeeze out 6-inch strips of dough into the hot oil. Fry until golden brown. Take out with a strainer and place on paper towels to drain off the excess oil. Sprinkle sugar over the *churros* to cover completely. Serve immediately.

Variation: *Churros* with No Milk

I have chosen the recipe above because it is the real *churros* taste I remember from my childhood in Cuba. It is also the one found on the corners of Miami, sold by street vendors. Other *churros* recipes vary, using 1 cup of water, no milk, and adding 2 eggs, one at a time, after the mixture forms a ball. Everything else remains the same.

Torrejas

French Toast in Syrup

Serves 6

Torrejas
2 eggs, beaten
¾ cup milk
½ tsp. cinnamon powder
3 tbsp. butter
6 slices bread

Sugar Syrup
¾ cup water
1 tsp. Spanish anise seeds
1½ cups sugar
¼ cup cooking wine (dry and/or white)

To prepare the **Torrejas,** mix the beaten eggs with the milk and cinnamon. In a skillet, melt the butter over medium heat. Dip each slice of bread into the milk/egg mixture, and fry in the skillet with the butter until golden brown on both sides. Place them on a serving plate.

To prepare the **Sugar Syrup,** boil the water with the anise seeds for 2 minutes. You should have about ½ cup of water left. Strain and discard the seeds. Add the sugar to that water, and boil for about 3 to 4 minutes. Remove from heat and add the cooking wine, stir, and pour over the *torrejas.*

Mantecaditos

Sugar Cookies-Cuban Style

These cookies are very easy to make, and children of all ages love them! They will be crispy, not chewy and soft.

Yields 16 to 18 cookies

2 cups all-purpose flour
¾ cup vegetable shortening
¾ cups sugar
1 egg
¼ tsp. salt
½ tsp. baking soda
Guava paste (optional)

Mix all of the ingredients together completely. Make a roll and cut ½-inch-thick slices to form the cookies. Press down on the slices with the palm of your hand. Dent the center of the cookie with your thumb and fill with guava paste if desired. Bake at 350 degrees for 20 minutes.

Guava Pie

Pastel de Guayaba

You can vary the filling in this pie. Try your favorite fruit paste or jelly. You may also use ham and cheese for a great breakfast pie!

Serves 6

2 cups all purpose flour
2 tbsp. sugar
1 tsp. salt
¾ cup vegetable shortening or butter
1 tbsp. rum or whisky
4 to 5 tbsp. water
14 to 16 oz. guava paste (do *not* use guava marmalade)
1 egg, beaten

Mix all dry ingredients well. Add the shortening and mix by hand or in a mixer equipped with dough blades. Add the rum; add the water a little at a time to form smooth, not sticky, dough. Form 2 balls with the dough. Using a rolling pin, roll out the dough on a clean countertop. Use plastic wrap under and on top of dough to avoid sticking. Form a 10-inch-wide circle from each ball of dough. Transfer to an 8- or 9-inch pie pan. Fill the pie with slices of guava paste. Do not worry if they are not perfect; they will even out when melted. Top with the other crust, and seal the edges by pinching them together. Brush the pie top with an egg beaten with a dash of sugar. Cut 4 slits on the top crust and bake in 350 degree oven for 20 minutes. Serve warm or cold.

Note: Do *not* use guava marmalade. You can use other fruit pastes and jellies in place of the guava paste. Whatever filling you choose should have a thick consistency.

Guava Shells in Heavy Syrup

Cascos de Guayaba en Almibar

Serves 5 to 6

8 to 10 ripe guavas
Dash salt
1½ to 2 cups sugar

Peel the guavas, and cut them in half lengthwise. Scoop out the seeds with the attached meat. Save for another recipe (such as **Guava Marmalade**).

Rinse the shells, and place them in a deep pot. Add water to cover the shells, plus a little more, and a dash of salt. Bring the water to a boil, lower the heat to medium, and cook the shells until somewhat tender but still firm. Add the sugar, stir to dissolve, and simmer until the syrup is thick and the shells are tender. Let cool and refrigerate. Serve with a thick slice of cream cheese.

Guava Marmalade

Mermelada de Guayaba

To save time and money, this recipe is usually done the same day as the **Guava Shells**. That way the inside of the fruit is used for the marmalade, and the shells for the other recipe.

Serves 8 to 10

8 to 10 ripe guavas
Dash salt
2 cups sugar

Peel the guavas, and cut them in half lengthwise. Scoop out the seeds with the attached meat/pulp. Save the shells for the **Guava Shells** recipe.

In a deep pot, boil the seeds with the attached meat/pulp in about 3 cups of water, with the dash of salt, for approximately 15 minutes. Let cool and blend in a food processor or blender—seeds and all. Strain with a large colander, and return to the pot. Add the sugar, and cook over medium/low heat until most of the liquid has evaporated and it has the consistency of a puree. Turn often with a wooden spoon. Serve with a thick slice of cream cheese. May be kept in the refrigerator for several days.

Papaya Chunks in Heavy Syrup

Fruta Bomba en Almibar

Serves 6 to 8

1 medium sized papaya (green or starting to turn yellow/orange)
1½ cup sugar (light brown recommended)
2 to 3 cinnamon sticks
1 tsp. vanilla extract
Dash salt

Peel the papaya and cut in half lengthwise. Spoon out all the seeds, and cut the pulp into chunks about 1 to 1½-inches in size. Place the papaya chunks in a 4- to 6-quart saucepot. Add enough water to cover the chunks, and boil over high heat for about 5 minutes. Drain and discard the water. Add enough fresh water to just cover the papaya chunks. Add the rest of the ingredients, stir to dissolve the sugar, and bring to a boil over medium/high heat. When the pot starts to bubble (boil), turn the heat to low. Simmer, uncovered, until the papaya is tender and the liquid is reduced and thickens into a heavy syrup. During this time, scrape the bottom of the pot gently with a spatula to prevent the fruit from sticking to the bottom. This process will only take 20 to 30 minutes, because the papaya fruit is very tender.

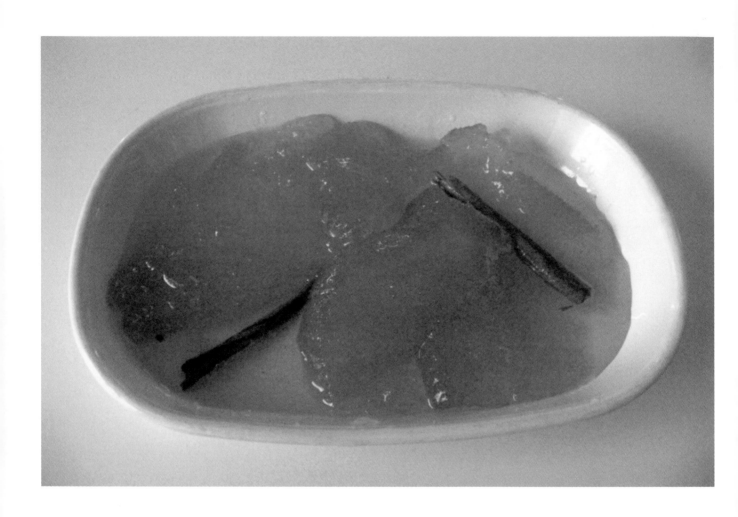

Grapefruit Shells in Heavy Syrup

Dulce de Toronjas

Serves 9 to 10

3 grapefruits (6 navel oranges may be substituted)
1 tbsp. anise seeds (Spanish anise)
2 cups sugar
½ tsp. lime juice
2 cinnamon sticks

Peel the grapefruits and cut in half lengthwise. Remove the grapefruit segments carefully with a thin, sharp knife. Save for a fruit salad, or to be eaten your favorite way. Cut the white meat under the peel lengthwise into segments. One large grapefruit should yield about 6 segments. Place in a bowl, and cover with water. Soak for about 2 hours, and discard the water.

In the meantime, boil one cup of water in a small saucepot. Add the anise seeds, and continue boiling for 3 minutes. Strain the liquid and save in a cup; discard the seeds. Place the grapefruit segments in a large pot fitted with a lid, and cover with water. Boil for about 5 minutes, and drain the water. Take out the grapefruits and rinse them with cool water. Press them firmly with both hands, squeezing out all the water from them. Place them back in the pot and repeat the process: boil for 5 minutes, drain, and squeeze out the water. Leave the segments on a platter the last time.

In the same pot, add approximately 8 cups of water. Add the cup of anise tea, the sugar, the lime juice, and the cinnamon sticks. Stir to dissolve the sugar, and wait for the water to boil. Add the grapefruit segments, placing them carefully in the pot. Cover the saucepot, and reduce the heat to medium. Cook for approximately 40 minutes. Uncover, and continue to cook for another 20 minutes or until the shells are tender and the syrup is thick. Check the shells often, pinching them with a fork and moving them carefully to avoid sticking to the bottom of the pot. Allow to cool. Keep in the refrigerator. Serve with a thick slice of cream cheese.

Mango Marmalade

Mermelada de Mango

Serves 6 to 8

3 cups mango pulp (very ripe)
2 cups water
2 cups sugar
1 cinnamon stick

Choose mangoes that are very ripe, with black spots already. Wash and peel the mangoes. Slice the pulp, leaving the seed as clean of meat as possible. Cut the meat (pulp) into chunks, and place in a food processor with the water. Puree on low speed, and transfer to a medium saucepan. Add the sugar and stir to mix completely. Add the cinnamon stick and turn the heat to medium/high until it starts to bubble (boil). Lower the heat and continue to simmer, half covered, stirring with a wooden spoon often. Cook over low heat for about 30 to 45 minutes, until it thickens to the consistency of a marmalade. Allow to cool. Serve with a thick slice of cream cheese. May be kept for days in the refrigerator.

White Sweet Potato Dessert
Boniatillo

The boniato is a sweet potato variety with dark pink skin and very sweet white meat. It is widely consumed by Cubans.

Yields about 10 *boniatillos*

Boniatillos
3 large boniato roots (white sweet potatoes), peeled and cut into chunks
½ tsp. salt
½ cup milk
2 tbsp. butter
Cinnamon powder

Heavy Syrup
½ cup water
½ tsp. Spanish anise seeds
2 pieces from an anise star
2 cinnamon sticks
1½ cups sugar

To prepare the **Boniatillos,** cook the boniatos in 3 to 4 cups of water with the salt and about 1 oz. (2 tbsp.) of milk. Bring water to a boil, reduce the heat to low, and simmer—half covered—for about 20 minutes or until tender. Drain any liquid left in the pot, and mash the boniatos with the butter and little splashes of the milk until creamy. If more liquid is needed, use liquid from the pot where they were cooked. Return to the pot, and mix in the heavy syrup.

To prepare the **Heavy Syrup,** boil the water with the anise seeds and anise star pieces and the cinnamon sticks for 3 minutes. You should have less than ¼ cup of water left. Strain and discard the cinnamon and anise seeds. Add the sugar to that water, moistening the sugar well. Boil for approximately 5 minutes, or until thick and reduced. Do not allow it to turn gold in color. Let cool, and add to the mashed boniatos.

Simmer the mashed boniatos and syrup, stirring constantly, until reduced and very thick. Sprinkle with cinnamon powder and stir. Transfer by spoonfuls to small paper cups, such as the ones for baking cupcakes, and let cool.

Beverages

Daiquiri

History of the Daiquiri

According to legend, in the beginning of the twentieth century, an engineer named Pagliuchi visited an iron mine called Daiquiri, located in the east of Cuba. At the end of a day of hard work, Pagliuchi suggested having a drink. The legend says that in the storeroom there were only rum, limes, and sugar. They mixed these ingredients in a shaker with ice.

"What is this cocktail called?" asked Pagliuchi.

"It has no name, so it must be a Rum Sour."

"No, that is not a worthy name for such a fine drink. We'll call it 'Daiquiri.'"

The rest is history.

The "Floridita" Daiquiri

It was probably Emilio González, a *cantinero* (bartender) of Spanish origin, who introduced the formula of the cocktail to the capital at the Havana Plaza Hotel. However, the person who made it famous was the bartender Constantino Ribalaigua Vert, El Grande Constante, in the bar where he worked—*El Floridita*—which was afterwards nicknamed, *La Cuna del Daiquiri* (The Cradle of the Daiquiri). According to some historians, one day Hemingway came into the bar to use the bathroom. When he came out, he was curious about the drinks he saw everyone enjoying so much. He tasted one and said, "It's good, but I prefer mine without sugar and double the rum."

Constante prepared it to his taste and served it to him saying. "There it is Papa." That's how a new cocktail was born: "the Papa Hemingway." Later, grapefruit juice was added to the recipe and it became the "Hemingway Special."

Regular Daiquiri

Serves 1

2 oz. light rum
1 oz. lime juice
1 tbsp. sugar
4 drops Maraschino
Cracked ice

Mix all the ingredients in a cocktail shaker or blender, and serve in a frosted wine glass.

"Hemingway Special"

Serves 1

2 oz. rum
2 oz. grapefruit juice
½ oz. Maraschino
½ oz. lime juice
Ice

Put all ingredients in a cocktail shaker or blender and mix well. Serve in a frosted cocktail glass.

Strawberry Daiquiri (Frozen)

Serves 1

3 large, ripe strawberries, cut in
   half (discard the leaves)
1 oz. lime juice
1 tbsp. sugar
2 oz. light rum
¾ cup ice cubes

Place all ingredients in a blender and process until it has the consistency of snow. Garnish with a strawberry on the rim of the glass.

Mojito

This is another world famous Cuban cocktail that was a favorite of Ernest Hemingway. He enjoyed drinking *mojitos* in *La Bodeguita del Medio,* a humble restaurant (still in existence) in Havana, Cuba.

Serves 1

6 to 8 mint leaves
1 oz. lime juice
2 tbsp. light brown sugar
1 thin lime wedge
2 oz. (¼ cup) dark rum (gold label or aged)
½ cup ice cubes
4 oz. club soda
1 nice sprig mint for garnishing

Place the mint leaves, lime juice, sugar, and lime wedge in a tall glass. Use a wooden muddle or a pestle to smash the mint leaves and lime wedge. Add the rum, ice, and club soda. Garnish with the mint sprig, and enjoy!

Note: I prefer to use the lime juice, with one small lime wedge, for added flavor. If several lime wedges are used instead of the juice, the bitter taste from the muddled lime peel is too overpowering.

Piña Colada

This is a tried and true recipe. It has the perfect balance of coconut, pineapple, and rum flavors.

Serves 4

3 cups pineapple juice
1 can cream of coconut (14 oz.)
2 cups light rum or 1½ cups light
rum and ½ cup spiced rum
2 cups ice cubes

Mix all ingredients, except ice, in a blender. Add ice and process until smooth and frosted. If the blender is not large enough, divide the batch in two portions after mixing the ingredients together but before adding the ice.

Note: The rum can be increased or decreased to suit your taste. The ice can also be increased to make it more "frozen" in texture.

Piña Colada Punch

Ponche de Piña Coco

A wonderful party punch! May be made "virgin" for a children's party by replacing the rum and champagne with lime soda, such as Sprite or 7-UP.

Serves about 24

1 large can pineapple juice (46 oz.), chilled
2 cans cream of coconut (14 oz.)
3 cups light rum
4 cups champagne, chilled
½ gallon pineapple sherbet
1 can pineapple chunks or tidbits (optional)

Combine all ingredients in a large punch bowl. Leave some pieces of the sherbet floating. If adding ice, this should be done at the time of serving.

Havana Sunrise

Amanecer Habanero

Serves 1

½ cup ice cubes
4 oz. orange juice
1 oz. light rum
1 oz. grenadine syrup

Place ice, orange juice, and rum in a tumbler, and stir. Add grenadine slowly without stirring.

Sangria

Sangria is a delicious wine cocktail that pairs well with all types of meats. It is originally from Spain.

Serves 6 to 8

6 cups red wine (Merlot or Cab-
  ernet Sauvignon)
1 can lime soda (Sprite, 7-Up,
  etc.)
½ cup brandy or rum
½ cup Triple Sec, Cointreau, or
  Grand Marnier
1 small apple, cored and chopped
1 lemon, thinly sliced with ends
  discarded
1 small orange, thinly sliced with
  ends discarded
Fruit cocktail, strained (optional)
Ice cubes

In a large pitcher, mix all the ingredients, stirring with a long wooden spoon.

Cuba Libre

Free Cuba

This name was given to this popular drink when the first Cuban exiles came to the United States.

Serves 1

4 oz. cola soda
1½ oz. dark rum
½ oz. lime juice

Place ice cubes in a tumbler. Add cola, rum, and lime juice. Garnish with a slice of lime.

Almond Mimosa

Mimosa de Almendra

Serves 2

½ cup chilled orange juice
1 cup chilled Champagne
1 oz. almond liqueur (such as Amaretto)

Use a red wine or brandy goblet. Pour the orange juice into the glass and add the champagne, stirring lightly. Lastly, pour the almond liqueur into the glass, but do not stir. Enjoy.

Note: I prefer mine with no ice, but crushed ice can be used if it is not cold enough for your taste.

Bull

Serves 2

1 12-oz. beer (regular beer works
   better than light)
1 cup ginger ale (lemon-lime sodas
   work well too)
1 tbsp. sugar
Juice from ½ lime
Ice cubes (about 1 cup)

Mix in a large pitcher or blender. The beer and soda will foam when mixed with the lime juice, so serve in tall glasses.

Coquito

Coconut Cream of Life

Serves 10 to 12 (small servings)

1 can coconut milk (14 oz.)
4 large egg yolks
1 cup white rum (or more to taste)
½ cup spiced rum
½ cup coconut rum
1 can condensed milk (14 oz.)
Cinnamon powder

Place all ingredients, except the cinnamon powder, in a blender and mix well. Pour in a bottle with a lid and refrigerate. Serve chilled in small liquor glasses. Sprinkle cinnamon powder on top after serving.

Variation: Better *Coquito*

Use the meat (pulp) from 1 dry coconut instead of the can of coconut milk. Mix with ½ cup of the rum in a blender, then strain through a cheese cloth, squeezing all the milk out; discard the coconut meat. This process works better if the pulp is divided into two batches.

Crema de Vie

Cream of Life

Crema de Vie is a Cuban-style eggnog, whose French name means "cream of life." It is a traditional after-dinner drink, commonly enjoyed during the holidays. It is usually homemade and found in almost every Cuban household during Christmas time. As with most Cuban desserts, it is extremely sweet and rich, and loved by young and old alike!

Serves 14 to 16

Simple Syrup
1 cup water
1½ cups sugar
2 or 3 cinnamon sticks
½ tsp. Spanish anise seeds

Crema de Vie
1 can condensed milk (14 oz.)
6 egg yolks
1 tbsp. vanilla extract
1 cup light rum (or more if desired!)

To prepare the **Simple Syrup,** boil the water and the sugar with the cinnamon sticks and anise seeds. Continue to simmer the syrup for about 10 minutes, until it is reduced to approximately 1¼ cups. Strain to take out the seeds and cinnamon sticks, and let cool.

To prepare the ***Crema de Vie,*** mix the rest of the ingredients with the syrup in a blender on a slow speed. Pour in a glass bottle with a cap and refrigerate. Serve chilled in small liqueur glasses. Keep refrigerated.

Chocolate Caliente

Hot Chocolate

Serves 3

1½ cups water
2 cinnamon sticks
1 can evaporated milk (12 oz.)
3 tbsp. unsweetened cocoa powder
½ cup condensed milk (14 oz.)
Dash salt
1 tbsp. cornstarch
Miniature marshmallows or whip-
    ped cream

In a 2-qt. saucepot, boil the water with the cinnamon sticks for about 3 minutes. Discard the cinnamon sticks, and add the evaporated milk to the water. Add the cocoa powder, condensed milk, and dash of salt. In a separate, small container, dissolve the cornstarch with a little water or cold milk (about ½ oz) until there are no lumps. Pour it slowly into the chocolate milk in the pot. Cook, stirring slowly with a wooden spoon, until the chocolate has thickened and it is hot. Do *not* overcook. Serve immediately. Place a few marshmallows in each mug, or add a spoonful of whipped cream on top.

Note: For an old-fashioned hot chocolate, use bitter chocolate tablets instead of cocoa powder, and follow the instructions on the package.

Cafe con Leche

Espresso Coffee with Milk

This is the breakfast drink for most Cubans. It is very easy to make. However, as with every recipe, there are individual touches that make them special.

Serves 1

Espresso coffee
¾ cup whole milk
2 to 3 tsp. sugar

Start with a good espresso coffee. It could be made from a fancy espresso maker, or an inexpensive Italian espresso maker for stovetop use. These are available in most Latin supermarkets, hardware stores, or pharmacies.

Heat the milk in a coffee mug in the microwave until very hot. Add the sugar and espresso coffee as desired, and stir well.

Note: For an old-fashioned *Cafe con Leche,* add 1 thin pat of real butter on top. For a creamier *Cafe con Leche,* use ⅔ part evaporated milk to ⅓ part water, instead of whole milk.

Ponche

Cuban-Style Eggnog

Serves 1

1¼ cup milk
2 cinnamon sticks
1 egg yolk
1 tbsp. sugar
Cinnamon powder
Nutmeg

In a 1-qt. saucepot, heat the milk with the 2 cinnamon sticks. Bring to a boil, lower the heat to medium, and simmer for about 3 to 4 minutes. In a large cup, beat the egg yolk and the sugar with a spoon until creamy. Add the hot milk to the egg yolk mixture and stir, mixing it well. Discard the cinnamon sticks. Sprinkle with cinnamon powder and a dash of nutmeg. Serve hot or warm.

Note: I prefer to strain the milk, after adding it to the egg, to remove any pieces of egg.

Manjar Blanco
White Nectar

The *Manjar Blanco* from Cuba differs greatly from that of other South American countries. This one is very similar to a vanilla pudding, but without the eggs and with less starch. It was traditionally given to children because it is nourishing without using eggs.

Serves 6 to 8

1 tbsp. cornstarch
4 cups milk
4 tbsp. sugar
2 tsp. vanilla extract
Cinnamon powder

Dissolve the cornstarch in about ½ cup of the milk, until there are no lumps. In a 2-qt. saucepot, heat the rest of the milk with the sugar and the vanilla extract. Pour the cornstarch mixture slowly into the pot, stirring with a wooden spoon until it thickens. The beverage will be slightly thick but not as thick as a pudding. Serve in small mugs or tea cups. Sprinkle cinnamon powder on top. May be served cold or hot.

Mango Shake

Batido de Mango

Serves 2

1¼ cup frozen mango pulp (meat) from fresh mango
1 cup whole milk
¼ cup condensed milk or 2 tbsp. sugar
Pinch salt

Choose a ripe mango with red/yellowish skin. If it has some black spots, that is even better. Peel the mango and cut into thick slices. Cut enough mango to make 1¼ cups of pulp. Place in a zip-lock bag and freeze overnight, or until hard. This process will allow for a better-tasting shake, because it will not be watered down with ice.

Place all ingredients in a blender, and process until smooth. Serve in a frosted glass. Decorate with a thin wedge of mango, slit and placed on the rim of the glass.

Variation: Fruity Mango Shake
For a really refreshing, fruity taste, try adding 1 cup of water, instead of milk, and 2 tbsp. of sugar, instead of condensed milk.

Mamey Shake

Batido de Mamey

This is Cuba's favorite shake. The mamey fruit has a brown, rough skin, with a bright, salmon-colored meat that is sugary sweet.

Serves 2

1½ cups frozen mamey pulp (from a fresh mamey fruit or frozen)
1½ cups whole milk
½ cup condensed milk
Pinch salt

If using a fresh mamey fruit, wait until it is perfectly ripe. Cut it in half lengthwise, discard the seed, and scoop out the pulp (meat). Discard the skin. Place the pulp in a zip-lock bag, and freeze until hard, usually overnight. This process will provide for a very cold shake without using ice, insuring a more flavorful, fruity taste.

In a blender, place all the ingredients and process on high, until smooth. If the shake becomes too thick, you may add a little more milk.

Papaya Shake

Batido de Fruta Bomba

Serves 2

1½ cups frozen papaya pulp (meat), from fresh papaya fruit
1½ cups whole milk
½ cup condensed milk or 3 tbsp. sugar

Choose a ripe papaya; the skin should be mostly yellow. Cut it lengthwise and scoop out the seeds with a spoon. Peel and cut into chunks; cut enough to make 1½ cups of pulp. Place in a zipper-close bag and freeze overnight, or until hard. This process will allow for a better-tasting shake, because it will not be watered down with ice. Place all ingredients in a blender, and process until smooth.

Champola de Guanabana

Soursop Shake

In some areas of Cuba, such as the Oriente province, the *champola* is different from a shake, because it is not made with milk. In their *champola*, the milk is replaced with water and sweetened with sugar, instead of using condensed milk. The taste is more "tropical" because it has a more naturally refreshing, fruity taste. However, in most areas of Cuba, *champola* is the same as a shake.

Serves 2

1¼ cups frozen guanabana (soursop) pulp
1 cup whole milk
½ cup condensed milk

Place all ingredients in a blender, and process on high until smooth. If the shake is too thick, add a little more milk. There is no need to add ice when using the frozen fruit pulp; this makes the shake creamier.

Note: Guanabanas are not easy to find in the United States. However, the frozen pulp is available in most supermarkets in large cities.

Orange Frost

Batido de Naranja

This is an easy and delicious way to boost your protein intake. Great for breakfast or a snack.

Serves 2

2 cups cold orange juice
3 scoops vanilla ice cream
2 tbsp. dry milk or small vanilla yo-
    gurt (high protein option)

In a blender, process the ingredients until smooth. Ice may be added.

Wheat Shake

Batido de Trigo

Serves 2

2 cups puffed wheat (found in cereal section of the supermarket)
2 cups whole milk
2 tbsp. sugar
1 cup crushed ice

In a blender, mix the first three ingredients until smooth. Add the ice, and process at the highest speed until frosted. If it is too thick, add a little more milk.

Peanut Butter Shake

Batido de Mani

Serves 1

1 cup milk
3 tbsp. smooth peanut butter
2 tbsp. sugar
2 scoops vanilla ice cream
¾ cup crushed ice (optional)

In a blender, process the first 4 ingredients until smooth. Add the ice, and blend at a high speed until frosted.

English Index

Spanish Index

R
Rabo Encendido, 151
Relleno de Arroz Blanco, 167
Ropa Vieja, 137
Ruedas de Papas y Cebollas, 197

S
Salmon a la Parrilla, 93
Salmon con Ruedas de Papas, 94
Sopa de Cherna, 71
Sopa de Garbanzo con Ternilla de Res, 65
Sopa de Platano, 73
Sopa de Vegetales en Crema, 70

T
Tamal en Hoja, 23
Tasajo, 153

Tiramisu, 233
Tocinillo del Cielo, 215
Torrejas, 243
Tortillas Mejicanas en Capas, 111
Tostones, 177
Tres Leches, 219

V
Vaca Frita, 135

Y
Yuca con Mojo, 187
Yuca Frita, 185

Z
Zarzuela de Mariscos, 80